His Last Queen

Margaret Draper

Also by Margaret Draper

Gloriana

Margaret Draper

His Last Queen

Margaret Draper

His Last Queen

First Published 2018

Copyright © 2018 by Margaret Draper

All rights reserved

Set in Calibri

This book is sold subject to the condition that it shall not, by way of trade or otherwise be lent re-sold, hired out, or otherwise circulated without the copyright holders prior consent in any form of binding or cover other than that in which it is published and without a similar condition including this condition being imposed on the subsequent purchaser.

His Last Queen

For Rosie – 'A Lass Unparalleled'

Margaret Draper

Contents

Chapter 1 Child Bride 9

Chapter 2 Young Widow 19

Chapter 3 The Pilgrimage of Grace 32

Chapter 4 A Royal Encounter 38

Chapter 5 Windsor Ball 46

Chapter 6 Enter Seymour..50

Chapter 7 Regina's Family...62

Chapter 8 The French Adventure 82

Chapter 9 Stepmother to Future King and Queens.................89

Chapter 10 Death of the King 99

Chapter 11 Leave the Court 103

Chapter 12 Sudeley Castle 113

Chapter 13 The Jealous Duchess 119

Chapter 14 The Queen in Print...140

Chapter 15 The Final Betrayal 148

Margaret Draper

Chapter 1   Child Bride

'No Mother, please no. Don't make me leave you'. Katharine sobbed in her mother's arms.

'You are fifteen years old now, or nearly so and it is time you found a good husband' said her mother gently. 'Now that I am a widow I must do what is best for you and what I think your father would have approved of. Do not forget that your father was a descendant of King Edward 111 and would have expected you to marry well and into the nobility I am sure. Your own godmother, whose name you bear is Queen Katherine of Aragon who is our honoured Queen still despite her present troubles and' she whispered 'is a true and staunch Catholic who thinks nothing of Luther or of any idea of divorce. Lord Borough is a good man and would you not think it a fine thing to live in Gainsborough Old Hall?'

'Am I never to see you again?' said Katharine, thinking how lonely she would be.

'Of course we shall meet again and we will write to each other every week'.

'I would have to say goodbye to William and Anne and my husband would be more like a grandfather. Why would he want to marry a young girl like me? He has children who live with him. Does he just want a younger servant? What about my little pony?'

'If you want your pony we can send him down but I think Lord Borough will mount you royally. In any case you are too big for him now and are riding a horse most of the time. You must not say those things again. Many young women would be honoured to be asked to marry into his family and he has done you the distinction of asking you. You should think sensibly Katherine. Do you want to be like your cousin Laura, left unwed in poverty? She turned down a good offer from Lord Bradben three years ago because she said she was too young at fifteen. She has not had another offer of marriage, her father is dead poor man and her mother is gravely ill. What will become of her? I hate to think. Lord Bradben is now like to die and would have left her a wealthy widow'. A few tears trickled down Katharine's cheek.

'I don't care how rich he is – I want to stay with you'.

'Come my dear, you would learn to love him and God would give you strength to be his comfort and helpmeet. You do not want to be an old maid and perhaps poor. I promise you that if you are so unhappy you can come back home although I very much hope that will not come to pass'. She lifted Katharine's chin and kissed her on the cheek, holding her close and stifling her own tears.

'I will do as you say Mother' said Katharine 'and will do my best to love him and serve his family'. Lady Parr sighed and held Katharine close to her. 'As soon as you feel settled and with your husband's assent, I will make the journey down to see you in your splendid new home. He is a good man and will look after you well and you will have a new family to call your own.'

'But you are my family and William and Anne are my family. Can I not stay here and look after you when you are old?'

'My very dear child that is not possible with me a widow. I must wed you where you will be somewhat more affluent than me.

Do not forget that I still have two other children to provide for and I must wed them where I know they will not want, if I can. These opportunities do not come along every day of the week.'

So Katharine reluctantly accepted her mother's arrangement and prepared to set out on a solitary journey into the unknown. Lord Borough wrote approving the plan and suggested that he and Katharine be married by proxy before she set out. She would love to have had a miniature portrait of her new husband but was afraid to ask for one. She wondered if he had the same misgivings and hoped he was not about to wed a fat and ugly wife rather than a comely and prepossessing one! It was not the wedding Katharine would have chosen with no husband by her side to see her wedding dress and to greet her tenderly. However her mother was a deeply religious person and Katharine trusted her to be making the wisest choice.

She wandered round her favourite haunts and walks thinking sadly that she might never see them again. Every place on their land brought back bitter sweet memories. It was here that she fell off her first pony when trying to jump a tree trunk. Over there was the secret hiding place where William had not been able to find her to her delight and his annoyance. Further on was the little wood, her favourite place for watching squirrels and their delightful young. Over there was the rock she sat on and wept her heart out when her father died. Turning back and sighing she wondered if life would ever be the same again. She talked late into the night with her sister Anne and speculated with her what it would be like to be married to an old man.

'I expect he might want a nurse for his old age' said Anne. 'But think how nice it will be to be mistress of your own house and your own destiny. I shall come and visit you and what a fine lady you will be! Will you expect me to curtsey to you?' asked Anne, stifling a giggle. The sisters put their heads together and laughed merrily. 'I shall expect you to be my lady in waiting and wait for orders which I shall give imperiously and which you will obey in fear and trembling'. The girls put their heads together and giggled till they ached.

'Oh Anne, I shall miss you every day' said Katherine trying to smile through her tears. William seemed less concerned and told his sister that he was sure they would meet again and that it was not as if she were going abroad. From that Katharine took little comfort, but then she thought William was unlikely to have to leave home to wed and would stay in the north where his home would always be.

Katharine reflected that the girls she knew locally who had married young had not made fine matches as she was assured this would be. Instead they had exchanged one life of varying degrees of hardship for another of the same, with the addition of growing families. One or two seemed to be content but she knew others who would gladly be wedding into a life of relative wealth and security instead of one of endless drudgery. Katharine had been brought up to be deeply religious like her parents before her and she said many a prayer to God to be with her and comfort her in her loneliness.

As Katharine prepared with her mother's help, the things she would take with her she reluctantly put to one side her childish dolls, her old friends, as being unsuitable sadly for a soon to be married young woman. She attended mass with her mother and siblings and asked permission to talk with the priest and ask his blessing. He counselled her as her mother had and told her that her Lord God had a mission for her to set an example of piety and holiness in her new household.

'You must show them that the people in the north are as devout and steadfast as any in other parts of the land.' He promised to write a prayer for her which would give her strength if she felt lonely. In the face of such support Katherine knew there was no turning back.

The day of departure came all too soon and wiping away the tears Katharine and her lady climbed onto their horses, the groom who was to accompany them straightened the bags on the pack animal and Katharine waved to her mother until she was a mere spot in the distance. She sadly watched the familiar landmarks slipping behind her until she left them all and entered new and unknown territory. The journey was long and often uncomfortable and involved four nights in wayside inns with their lumpy and itchy beds and indifferent food. The countryside became flatter and greener and the beloved hills of her childhood were no more. The first night she cried herself to sleep quietly and then was awakened by the sharp bites of the bed bugs. She became absorbed in catching them but was not quick enough to crush them between her fingers. She dined off mostly plain and sometimes unpalatable food and after her mother's wholesome cookery this added to her misery. The innkeepers were not aware of her destiny, nor would she push herself to complain. She rather thought they were taking advantage of her tender years and was afraid to show her innocence. She told herself that this would not last more than three or four days and then she would be looked after in the style to which she was accustomed.

More interesting was the countryside which mellowed the further south she went. If it lacked the rugged beauty she had grown up with she would not dwell on it. Nevertheless she did miss the hills.

As they all entered the long drive at the Old Hall she and her lady looked with pleasure at the beautiful parkland which she must now call home. Happily the sun broke through the clouds and seemed to welcome her to her new life. She had dearly loved the country round her old home but this was grander, the oak trees older and larger and the hall itself was more imposing than any dwelling she had seen at home. The grey stone walls rose impressively and were topped by a fine tower and lookout.

'Am I really to be mistress here and why me?' she wondered. Lord Borough was awaiting her in the great hall and greeted her warmly, introducing his children who looked to Katharine to be older than her mother. She thought he looked more aged than she had imagined but he was gracious and obliging and obviously taken with his new wife. She gazed around the hall in wonder at the walls covered with shields and pikes, catching the light from the huge welcoming fire. She realised Lord Borough was watching her and smiling and she remembered her mother's axiom that it was rude to stare. For the first time in several days she felt warm and cosy. She was introduced to Lord Borough's son Thomas and his wife Agnes whose own brother was married to Lord Borough's daughter. It seemed to her a very close knit family and that she was an unknown outsider. However, Agnes was delighted to welcome her and she felt sure that she would have a friend in her and a guide to help her. She was correct in her instincts and Agnes indeed remained a friend and ally to the end of her days.

'You will see our three children tomorrow' said Agnes with a warm smile. 'They are so looking forward to meeting you and showing you their school books. I have three boys who are inclined to tease but mean well'. 'I have a brother and am used to teasing' said Katherine with a little smile. 'When you are settled in you may like to sit in on some of their lessons?' Katharine nodded her approval as she had been keenly interested in learning since her early years and was eager to pass on her knowledge with their tutor's permission. Her feelings lifted as she saw in this a way to still her aching heart. She knew that she would feel more at home with children than adults and felt a bit guilty for those sentiments.

  Agnes took Katharine to her apartment with its fine views over the rolling parkland planted with magnificent old oak trees and she told her that when she was ready she should come down where there would be a meal awaiting her. Although very tired after the long journey Katharine smiled her thanks and thought that perhaps after all she might be contented with such welcoming people. After a meal of venison from the parkland and a delicious syllabub, Katharine curtseyed to her new family and begged leave to retire early to rest before the morrow. She wondered what they would say about her when she was gone but was not going to try to eavesdrop. Her mother had told her that eavesdroppers never heard anything good about themselves.

When she eventually lay on the vast bed she fell immediately into a dreamless sleep. In the middle of the night she woke suddenly and was aware of the heavy curtains which had a different but not unpleasant smell from those at home. She was wide awake and alert when she heard loud snores coming from the dressing room and she crept out of bed to investigate. Lord Borough lay on the bed with his mouth open, deeply asleep which she thought was very obliging of him.

She was awoken in the morning by her husband standing by her bedside and parting the curtains. 'What are you doing here in my bed?' he asked querulously. 'I had to sleep in the dressing room which is not very comfortable'. Katharine was almost lost for words but replied quietly

'I thought it was my bed too sir'. He grunted and stumped off saying nothing. Her heart sank at this encounter.

'He is mad' she thought to herself. 'Did everyone but me know this? Did my mother know? Did Agnes know?' Once more the sickening feeling pressed against her ribs. How was she expected to cope with this? Was she wedded to a lunatic? There had been a mad old woman living not far from her in the north and at first Katherine had avoided her in fear. However as she knew her a little better she found her friendly if strange and certainly not a cause for fear. Perhaps this would be the same.

When, with her lady's help she had attired herself for the new day she set off along the dark corridor to find the hall of the previous evening. As she came to a window along the corridor she paused and took in the pretty parkland view. Its pleasant undulations and mighty oaks promised happy hours of exploration on horse or foot. She imagined she could ride as far as she liked without leaving the grounds and for the first time appreciated the advantages of being a fine lady. It was not going to be too bad! Waiting by the fire was Lord Borough who stepped forward and bowed to her kissing her hand and asking how long she was staying. Katharine was bereft of an answer as she caught Agnes's sympathetic smile.

'I am your wife Lord Borough' she said quietly. Lord Borough looked puzzled and then took her hand and kissed it again.

'Then I hope you will be very happy here. Do you like riding? I have a nice little mare, very quiet that you may like to try'. He sidled up to her and whispered 'I had a wife you know but she is gone now. She is buried in the chapel' he said sadly.

'I have heard that is so my Lord, indeed I have and I am very sorry for it. I hope you will show me her resting place where I will say a prayer.' She looked up at him and he gave her a beatific smile. 'Perhaps one day I may explore the park with you if you would be my guide. However I am afraid I do not hunt'.

'Never mind my dear, we will teach you to hunt like my wife'. Katharine thought it wiser not to reply to that remark and curtseyed her thanks instead. She was puzzled by Lord Borough but realised that at his age it was no doubt normal to be confused sometimes. After all he was nearly four times her own age. He seemed kindly and well disposed towards her and she had Agnes to help her out of difficult situations. Agnes was only too happy to have a young companion and after breakfast took Katharine to meet her children and their tutor. Here Katharine felt at home and she took a keen interest in the boys' education without interfering which won the tutor to her side. Part of the lesson was a question and answer time which was all spoken in Latin and which Katherine deduced was about religious services. She reflected that if anyone was to be instructed in this company it was more likely to be herself than the boys. Their teacher was very strict with them and made them recite long passages from memory. He then quizzed them about Roman Britain and Julius Caesar which was something completely new to Katharine but fascinating. She reflected that her own education had had more of religion and religious practices in it than history. After an hour of listening Katherine slipped out before she had to answer any questions herself! She made her way back to the great hall where Lord Borough was seated by the fire awaiting her with a kindly smile.

In his lucid moments Lord Borough was eager to tell Katharine the history of the hall and took pride in the fact that both Richard 111 and Henry V111 had stayed there. He knew that Katherine's father was descended from King Edward 111 though Katherine herself had not mentioned that fact. He must, she thought with amusement, have enquired about her ancestry at some stage.

'King Henry liked his food and was inclined to indulge himself. However he seemed to enjoy his visit and loved to hear about the history of the region and the hall. He especially liked to hunt and wanted nothing else in the way of exercise. However we had some difficulty in borrowing a horse that was up to weight.' Lord Borough was kind and thoughtful though Katharine sometimes found him looking at her with a puzzled expression in his eyes.

'Where did we first meet my dear?' he asked and Katharine gently replied that her initial meeting was here at the hall which seemed to amuse him.

Katherine resolved to take to her new surroundings and family despite Lord Borough's distracted remarks. He treated her as any honoured guest rather than a wife and from the odd remarks Katharine heard about him she realised he was still held in high esteem despite his memory lapses. Sometimes he asked her where she lived and Katharine replied that that she was born in the north of England and brought up in Kendal. When he enquired after her family she replied that her mother was still alive of course and very much looking forward to meeting him.

'I have never been to the north' said Lord Borough, 'but if people are as delightful and friendly as yourself I have obviously been remiss'. Katherine swept him a low curtsey and sat beside him by the fireside.

Chapter 2 Young Widow

What Katharine enjoyed most of all was sharing the lessons of her 'grandchildren' and trying to help them with their work afterwards. Her mother had imbued her with deeply religious feelings and these she was keen to pass on to the boys, even if they were not as receptive as she might have wished. Once when she opened her grammar book with them sitting beside her the boys looked at each other behind her back with a bored expression. She caught a glimpse of their faces and smothered a smile.

 'After this we will go and practise your archery' she said much to their relief. 'However' she added 'You must persevere with your Latin studies so that you may read the word of God'. Katharine had little Latin and no Greek so could not help them. Word was about that the Bible was being translated into English but she had yet to see a longed for copy. The boys were mischievous but never malicious and treated Katharine like an older sister rather than a new grandmother. They delighted in showing her round the home farm with its cows and sheep and even peeped in with her at the bull 'Giant' who turned his huge head round and snorted terrifyingly at them, stamping his foot. Clouds of steam rose from his back which made him seem more threatening than ever. Together with the boys she scampered back to safety laughing merrily. If she missed her brother and sister, these young boys filled the gap and softened the home sickness which slowly melted away.

In quiet moments she would make her way to the beautiful little family chapel where she could give thanks for her new family and pray for her old one. She offered prayers and gratitude to God that they were all so kind and understanding of her years. She often stopped by the beautiful tomb of the late Lady Borough and wondered what sort of a lady she had been. She pondered the effect her death had had on her husband and wondered if all spouses were as affected as he seemed to be. Her own mother must have been equally devastated but she was sane and bright despite her loss.

She persevered with her Latin in order to study the Bible but in truth she found that language as difficult as did her charges. Although she heard the language in church she had to confess that not all of it made sense to her. Her difficulties made her even more sympathetic to the schooling of the boys, but recalling her mother's admonitions she determined never to embrace defeat.

However the strange marriage was not to last long and it was not many months before Lord Borough became seriously ill and took to his bed most of the time. He seemed to think that Katharine was hired to nurse him and she did not disillusion him.

'What is your name?' he asked once and she replied 'I am your helpmeet Katharine'.

'No, no I fear you are mistaken. My wife died some time ago. I cannot remember when exactly but she did not look like you at all.' Katharine smiled fondly at him and did not attempt to argue. He did not pursue the matter and she would sometimes pray with him but he soon tired of that. She would sit by his bedside and encourage him to share his memories of days at court and his skill at jousting in his youth. She asked him about King Henry and listened with interest to his reminiscences.

'The King was a fine, strong man in his young days and in many ways still is' he said. 'He used to carry a token of his lady love of the day pinned to his jerkin and if he won he would put the token on the end of his spear and gallop round with it. Of course he was already married to Queen Katharine of Spain but she had to put up with his championing of other ladies. Then he would halt in front of his lady and bow to her and blow a kiss and then ride up to the Queen and bow to her and blow another kiss. He was tall, over six feet, with red-gold hair and he was indeed very handsome to the ladies.'

'Did Queen Katherine not object to His Majesty blowing a kiss to another lady?' she enquired.

'No, no she was far too wise for that!' smiled Lord Borough. 'Anyway he was in love with the Queen and she with him and she was wise enough to tolerate his pride. It does not do to contradict or argue with the King. Don't ever forget that' and Katherine thought she would have no difficulty in following his precept if she ever met the King. Once he asked her about life in the north of England and whether it was cold and rainy all the time. Katharine would wipe away a tear unobserved and paint a picture of the northern hills with their sheep and the valley meadows with their corn and their cows. She was heartened that he had remembered that she had come from the north and that perhaps his memory was returning.

'Do you never long to return to the north?' he once asked her and she sat quietly for a few minutes before replying. 'Indeed my Lord I sometimes long to go back but chiefly to see my mother and my brother and sister. I loved the hills especially at sunset when the deep golden sun sank behind them. But' she added raising a smile for him 'it is much warmer and gentler here and although there are no hills to speak of, the country is soft and welcoming and grows on me day by day. I love to watch the fields of corn waving in the wind and am sorry to see them cut to the ground'. Her husband smiled gently and stretched his hand out to cover hers. He asked her to fetch a small box which lay at the bottom of a cupboard in the corner. He opened the box and took out a necklace with a large emerald on a gold chain. 'This is for you Katharine. It belonged to my late wife'. Katherine was so surprised at his clearness of brain that she could not find words to thank him. She leant over and kissed him warmly and he held her close and smiled in contentment.

'Sometimes I forget things and people think I am distracted. But I know that you are my young wife and that you are very kind to me. I have not long to live and I also know that your gentle presence has brought me much joy'. Katherine at this could not hold back the tears try as she might and the dying husband and his gentle young wife held hands in the fading light where Katharine's tears were not so much in evidence. Although he sometimes seemed to forget that Katharine was his wife, he always treated her with kindness and relished her companionship. Sometimes he asked her to sing to him as he lay with his eyes closed as she quietly hummed and sang the songs she had first heard at her mother's knee.

His eventual sudden death left her a wealthy widow at the age of eighteen. She was sad to lose Lord Borough as he had been like a kind uncle to her and as long as she humoured him all had been peace and quiet. She was comforted by his family and she in turn tried to comfort them. They had a small private funeral mass in the family chapel and Lord Borough was laid to rest there as he had wished beside his first wife.

She stayed on for some time in the Hall to which she was now attached but felt herself to be an unnecessary adjunct to life under the new Lord Borough. Eventually she decided that she would return to her mother and say farewell to the Borough family who had been so kind to her, but the news reached her that her mother had unexpectedly died in her absence. Alone in the world as it seemed to her she wandered in the parkland wondering what course she should take. If she stayed on what would her position be and how long could she bear it however kind the family were? She prayed for guidance but none came to relieve her jangled mind.

However that was not the end as fate held another card in store, for some months later she received an offer of marriage unexpectedly from Lord Latimer of Snape Castle in Yorkshire. He had been a friend of her mother's for some years. Lord Latimer was still only in his late thirties and was a member of the powerful Neville family who had had Plantaganet connections and been close to the throne. He had had two wives who were now deceased. She was attracted by his offer as a return to her northern roots and after much soul searching prepared herself for her new life though very sad to leave the place she had grown to love as her home. She had long talks with Agnes who was agreeable to her new offer.

'We shall not lose touch dear Katharine. You have been a wonderful new mother or I should say 'grandmother' to the boys and they will never forget you. You gave my dear late father-in-law much contentment in his last years. We shall think of you often and we shall certainly meet again'. How true this remark turned out to be!

Katharine wept at the kind words but saw the wisdom of Agnes's thoughts. In fact she had confided in Agnes previously when she was torn between an unknown destiny and a more certain future where she knew she would be welcome. However the thought had constantly come to her during the night watches that she might outstay her welcome here and that to start again might be wiser. She had considered living in the north alone as an independent woman but realised the potential difficulties of a wealthy young lady and the unwelcome attentions she might attract in that capacity.

'You must come north as my first visitors as soon as I get settled dear Agnes. In fact I could have felt an unwelcome intruder here but that never, never happened. Thank you for all your kindness.' She said a tearful farewell to the boys and was touched to see their sad faces. They had between them carved a creature which looked somewhat like a bull with sharp horns and a ring in his nose. 'This is a reminder of your friend Giant' they said and she hugged them warmly. 'I hope you did not cut your fingers making this for me' she smiled and they shook their heads but kept their hands hidden.

'We shall have no-one to tease Giant with or to ride in the park with' they said to Katherine. She was touched by the kindness of the boys which she thought unusual for those so young. In truth the parting from the Boroughs was far from easy but her life with them had made her grow up quickly and had given her the confidence of a young adult.

So Katharine embarked on her new adventure and sometime around 1533 she became the third Lady Latimer marrying a debonair and gracious lord with Catholic sympathies although her own covertly leaned towards the new and simpler faith that she had heard of. In a time of flux in religious affiliations it was wise to conform to the favoured type of religion. Katharine, for all her youth, realised that the practice of religion was in a time of upheaval and that deeply held beliefs were often best kept personal. What was the accepted practice today might be the anathema of tomorrow until things settled down. Luther had caused much uncertainty throughout Europe and wise people tended to follow their religion quietly rather than challenging the existing observances.

Katharine set off for the north with both hope and misgiving. On leaving the Hall she kept looking back waving whilst shedding tears until her old family were out of sight. As she journeyed north the landscape became more hilly and her heart began to lift within her. Although she felt apprehension about her new husband she felt joy at the thought of returning to the north of England. She hoped indeed that Lord Latimer would be of sound mind as he was so much younger than Lord Borough.

Snape Castle was a very different home from Gainsborough Old Hall and from the outside looked as grey and grim and forbidding as a fortress. It did not have the homely charm of Gainsborough but her welcome was just as warm. Lord Latimer seemed delighted to welcome her to his ancestral home when he came out to greet her.

'You are very welcome to the north again' he smiled and led her into the Hall. 'This castle may not look like a home from the outside but it has had to defend itself on more than one occasion and so the appearance of a fortress explains its history. If the Scots decide to come south we think we are well able to defend our fortress home'.

Within it was more welcoming and warm though rather dark and the portraits on the walls looked unfriendly and stern.

'I will tell you in time who all these rather fearsome people are' Lord Latimer said with a smile. 'Perhaps they had good reason to look so stern and unwelcoming, but do not fear they cannot step out of their frames to upbraid us'. Katharine smiled at her new lord and thought it was a fine thing that he could comment thus on his ancient forbears. She felt that she liked him already and that this liking would happily turn to love as she grew more familiar with his ways. In time he broached the subject of her mother and said he had seen her not long before her sudden death. He said to Katherine's pleasure that her mother had said that she had heard nothing but good from the life Katharine had led with her last family though he never asked her about the Norfolk days out of consideration for her sadness. Katharine was appreciative of his sensitivity and as time went by the memory of Gainsborough Old Hall became dimmer and more remote.

'After you have rested we will dine and then if you are not too fatigued we will celebrate your safe arrival with a mass in the chapel' he said. Katharine was agreeable to this arrangement and was not unhappy to follow the old religion of her mother in this house too. Whatever preferences she may have and however much she admired the stance of Luther, she decided that the gates of heaven could be reached by more than one path and that her personal leanings should be held in abeyance for the sake of marital harmony. As she knew her new lord better perhaps he would be amenable to the new practices which were on the rise. When she felt more settled she asked Lord Latimer about his most recent contact with her late mother and how he had heard about her death.

'Your mother sadly seemed to catch some sort of infection though whence it came it is not clear. Her lady did not have it although there was a similar illness in the next village I was told.

I asked her about her family and she told me that you were widowed not long since so I took the liberty of contacting you. Your dear mother did not suffer and died quietly in her sleep.' This was an enormous relief to Katharine and she could begin to put her uncertainties to one side. In the middle of the night when her husband was asleep she thought about her departed mother and wept silently. She did not want Lord Latimer to think her sad and ungrateful but she never forgot her mother especially in the small hours of the night. She vowed to visit her grave one day if possible.

It seemed that news travelled quickly despite the limited means of communication and Katharine was relieved to know from her old home that her dear mother had not had a long illness as Lord Latimer had confirmed and had had her daughter Anne with her to the end. William had been away from home for he was living with a noble family as was often the case at that time.

The sensitive problem of religious differences between the old religion and the new Anglicanism had been bubbling up for some time following King Henry's defiance of the Pope over his protracted divorce proceedings from Katherine of Aragon. He had declared himself King of the new English church and Roman Catholic practises obeying the Pope were officially frowned on. Although Henry never again called himself a Roman Catholic he was to the end of his days a Catholic but an English Catholic nevertheless. In the north change was not received so willingly as it seemed to be in the south. Many people silently still regarded themselves as subjects of the Pope but it was wiser not to air that view.   Not long after the time of Katharine's second marriage matters came to a head in 1636 in the north where old practices died hard and where there was a tenacious adherence to Catholicism and monastic orders with all their wealth, which defied change. Katharine had a powerful reminder of this not long after she became the new mistress of Snape Castle.

When she was in her room with her personal maid and was looking through her belongings she came across the rosary of Queen Katherine of Aragon which had been gifted to her mother at Katherine's christening, for she had long been a friend of the Queen and had asked the Queen to be her daughter's godmother. Katharine treasured it and handled it often with its sweet reminders of her late mother and the divorced Queen. She took it out and kissed it and then showed it to her maid.

'This is my most treasured article which was used by Queen Katharine and given to Mother'. To her astonishment her maid fell on her knees and then prostrated herself on the floor.

'Do get up Mary. Why are you doing that?'

Crossing herself the maid replied 'That is a sacred possession madam of our most holy and rejected Queen a true Catholic as she was and is and nobody can say that's not true'. Katharine was taken aback by the vehemence of her reaction but gradually by careful questioning she learnt that the ordinary people of the area were true Catholics and wanted no truck with the new religion or a new queen.

'Like our lord we revere the old religion and ....'

'Hush, say no more. I understand how you feel but it is not wise to talk as you do'. Katharine turned this little scene over in her mind when left alone and realised that old habits died hard and that the north of England disliked change and the actions of the King and his minister

Cromwell. They still revered the Pope despite his quarrel with the King. There was, however, a growing unrest with the 'rape' of the monasteries and the seizure of its plate instigated by Cromwell acting for the King who eyed its wealth and influence enviously. There was a growing divide between the conservative north of the country and the people in the south. The King had had long conversations with Cromwell.

'I see this wealth belongs to the Pope and not to myself' said the King. ' What do you say Cromwell?'

'Indeed the monasteries send much money to Rome which should rightly stay in the mother country' replied Cromwell.

'This will not do Cromwell. The Pope is taking what is due to us here. What do you suggest?' And of course, Cromwell said what his master wanted him to say.

'It would be well that the monasteries were relieved of their surplus wealth Your Majesty' he said.

'And how do you suggest that this is done?' demanded the King.

'It would be as well for the monasteries to send us an inventory of their riches and we will decide how much they really need' said Cromwell. 'If they choose to object we can raise the monasteries to the ground and so much the worse for their intransigent priests.'

The King rubbed his chin and considered how much opposition he would meet. The monks would not be armed and in any case their religion forbade physical violence. It should be an easy way to enrich the royal coffers and keep the monasteries in their proper place.

Both he and Cromwell saw the wealth of the monasteries as an easy supply of funds and Henry spied the advantage of robbing the wealth of the monks whilst at the same time constraining the power of his old enemy Rome and lining his coffers. He thought with grim satisfaction of the annoyance to the Pope but felt no remorse as he considered that the Pope's power should be restricted to his immediate domain. There were those at court who would have liked to beg him to desist but he was not about to consider their feelings and they knew better than to oppose him. The people of the north, being more conservative than the south were not reluctant to see some wealth garnered but they did not want the monasteries to be dissolved and its monks scattered as Henry was inclining towards in the thirties. Trouble was brewing and religion was once again underlying the contest.

When Lord Latimer came in later in the day Katharine lost no time in describing the scene with her maid and asked him if feeling was really so strong. He walked around the room considering and then asked Katharine to sit beside him whilst he informed her about the growing unrest and danger that threatened the country.

'King Henry is loved by many and feared by others. However he has Cromwell by his side urging him on and it is he who is at the root of all this desecration of the holy monasteries. I fear great trouble. I have just come back from a meeting of people of all walks of life who are determined to march on London and beg the King to stop his minister in his tracks. I am one of the leaders' he said quietly.

Katherine was too shocked to speak for a time but then asked him what danger he would be in.

'That I do not know but you will be safe here with my steward and men to guard you. I cannot risk my eternal soul by not protesting' he said. 'But you must not worry about me. I have been chosen to lead this protest to London because it is thought that the King might take notice of a person like myself who has often met him. He knows that I respect him highly and would let no harm come to him but that I must make my voice heard for Mother Church. Pray for me daily Katherine and pray to see me back soon.'

Once convinced of his mission he said a tender farewell to Katharine and gave her his blessing which made her weep bitter tears.

'You are in good hands and you can trust my guards to take care of you' he said kissing her gently. 'As soon as I have news and whenever I can I will write to you and I shall be back soon'.

He mustered the northern rebels and led them into Doncaster and York recruiting sympathisers along the way. There he took part in the Great Council of the Pilgrims and asked whether subjects might not 'move war in any case against their prince', an inflammatory question at that time. He knew the King and the extent of his powers and the fact that he was willing to confront him showed the passion of his religious beliefs.

Chapter 3 The Pilgrimage of Grace

Latimer set off within days followed by his ramshackle army gathering supporters along the way and cheering greetings as he went. It was as well that most onlookers were behind him because his contingent often depended on them for food. As he went further south the shouts of well-wishers thinned out and the feeling against the King's actions was less vocal. Sometimes he had to call a halt approaching a village as the locals were suspicious of his intentions and he was obliged to explain his mission. He was met with some agreement and also a degree of scepticism as to his possible fate but he persevered with his loyal followers until he reached Whitehall. On explaining his mission he was, after a lengthy interval, summoned by the King. With a subdued heart at his impending fate he went to face the reckoning. However the King was not there and he was to his dismay immediately conveyed under guard to the Tower to shiver and face the rats and Cromwell who, the next day was careful not to soil his scarlet robes on his visit and held them fastidiously close to him.

'Lord Latimer' he purred whilst watching his prey with slit eyes. 'I am indeed sorry to find you here when you need not be. The King sends his good wishes though his affairs of state preclude a meeting with him. However, he wonders why you should lead an army which has already capitulated. Your men are forgiven as they are unlettered farm workers and are already setting off for home with an escort for several miles. I have promised them there shall be no more trouble for them in the north. You, yourself are at liberty to return home if you will do me a favour. Our beloved church in Westminster is sorely in need of funds and the King asks you to honour your long standing pledge to help mother church. Of course if you choose not to you may find life more difficult and infinitely more dangerous for yourself. If you agree you are free to go home tomorrow. If you choose to stay you will have no-one to fight with here. Consider how forgiving our gracious King can be and how willing he is to overlook this incident'. He withdrew a letter from his sleeve and handed it to Latimer who took it with some misgiving.

'We look forward to meeting your new wife before too long.' wrote the King. I trust that this error of judgement will not be repeated and that peace will be restored in the north'.

'May I be permitted to speak to my retainers who remain?'

'They are not here Lord Latimer. They were shown the gallows at Tyburn where they would undoubtedly be hanged or they could be granted the King's mercy and some recompense for obedience with their promise of no more unrest in the north. They chose the latter' he smiled and glanced round the cell with a faint shiver.

Lord Latimer, realised he was cornered but promised to give his answer on the morrow. Cromwell sniffed and then smiled and left. He pondered on the import of the Cardinal's words and called in a guard to find out the truth of his army's desertion on promise of payment. He had to wait until the next day to have the Cardinal's words confirmed and realised he had no choice but to return home.

However he had escaped recrimination and he was able to leave the Tower and begin the return journey north much to Katherine's relief and joy.

Katharine in the castle had not committed herself to the rebel cause and remained aloof from the revolt. She was possibly influenced by the intervention of their reforming neighbour

Bigod, whose son was to marry her step daughter and was beginning to quietly espouse the reforming cause which had long held an interest for her. The mystery remains as to how Lord Latimer escaped with his life and how the Latimers continued to live at peace with their neighbours in the north and in amity with the King in the south. Lord Latimer must have been a person of magnetic personality to continue to be on good terms with both the reforming monarch and his own diehard Catholic neighbours. If money changed hands to facilitate his release so soon there remains no proof as yet discovered

Four days previously in Snape Castle whilst Latimer was in the south, news of the activities had filtered through to Katharine and she heard the extraordinary tidings of her husband having been imprisoned and then released and ordered to control his previous supporters in the north. She was both puzzled at the turn of events and alarmed. The local northern people also formed their own opinion that Latimer had been suborned by the court and they prepared to storm Snape Castle and capture its occupants as hostages. The first she heard was a commotion at the bridge and then shouts and yells as the main door of the castle was broken down with a ram. Into the room where she sat, terrified, burst the insurgents who confronted her boldly.

'Lady Latimer' they said with some menace 'as long as you stay quiet you will come to no harm'.

'What are your intentions?' she asked trying to sound unmoved by their malice.

'We are here to take an inventory of your goods for future reference'.

'But why would you do that? You know Lord Latimer is the local leader of the Pilgrimage'.

'No more he is my lady' said they. 'Once he was our leader, now he is our foe. He has been deputed by the King to act for him and we have decided to itemise his goods for subsequent sequestration'.

'But that cannot be! My lord is by now at the head of his army in London'.

'No madam you are misinformed. He has turned against us and we do not regard him as a leader. His militia were threatened and then released on condition that they returned for the north immediately. The King made peace with Lord Latimer on certain conditions and one was that he return home immediately on pain of his life – somewhat repentant it seems. He should be back in a few days.'

Katharine tried to gather herself together with some dignity and watched with dismay as the men roamed through the house itemising the furnishings and valuables and perhaps pocketing some of the smaller treasures but happily not finding her reliquary of Katherine of Aragon.

However they did no harm to the residents of the castle to Katharine's relief and after a noisy and frightening afternoon they left posting guards on the gate and promising to return but leaving her unmolested and deeply worried. She sent a messenger to her neighbour Bigod as follows:-

'I have heard that John has spent a night or two in the Tower of London and that our neighbours who supported him have returned home without success. John has been released on payment of a heavy fine. What is happening with you?'

Bigod replied by one of his servants –'I have been left unmolested but have been questioned about my allegiances. All is well here but I cannot leave the house at the moment'.

Katherine's maid Mary dissolved in hysterics when they threatened her with a body search which fortunately they did not carry out as long as she quietened down.

Katherine eagerly awaited the safe return of her husband and gave thanks in the chapel for his extraordinary escape. A week later he turned up at the Castle as she realised when she heard the raised voices outside which gradually tempered their volume into a buzzing conversation. After what seemed like an eternity he entered the castle alone, travel stained and weary.

'Oh my dear John' sobbed Katharine. 'You can hardly imagine what a time we have had and how I have worried about you'. Latimer held her close and calmed her sobs.

'It has indeed been a dreadful time and we must hope all will be peaceful now. The King has promised not to disturb the monasteries in the north any more and he has spared my followers from a horrible death. I cannot blame them for abandoning me as they were shown the gallows at Tyburn and it was suggested that they may prefer to be burnt. I was housed in the Tower for two nights which was an unspeakable experience and was relieved of much money. The King has shown mercy to me and to them for which I have to be grateful. How have you fared?'

Katherine replied that the contents of the house had been subject to an inventory and that it had been a frightening experience which was thankfully over now. 'They did not take anything of value although they caused much distress and weeping. I thank God for your safe return. The guards you left to defend the Castle were overcome by numbers though they were later released. The attackers did not harm us but made us stay in one room whilst they roamed round the house making an inventory of the contents. It was all very intimidating but no damage was done to us. They didn't take anything of great value.'

'I have had to pay a heavy fine levied by Cromwell for the repair of churches' he said. 'We are alive but poorer I have to say. Now we must repair relations with our neighbours as best we can'.

'But what about the monasteries and the poor monks thrown out into the cold?'

'We must do our best for them – we have room here and we must learn to live side by side with them and the reformers. Things are changing in England and the King has old debts to settle with the Pope. We are promised a peaceful life as long as we do not cause trouble and we follow our own path in peace'. It was a bitter pill for Latimer to swallow but in time he learnt to live with the new and strange order. In her own mind Katherine had pondered the conversations with her neighbour Bigod and he had talked much of the new Anglicanism which worshipped more simply and without the elaborate rituals of the old religion. The King would replace the Pope as head of the English Catholic church and that in itself he thought would be welcomed. The people would come round to it with some persuasion although he did not elaborate on what sort of persuasion that might be. She turned over Bigod's sayings and thought she saw a way which she could follow in its simplicity and freedom from the Church of Rome.

The resentments which had brewed and bubbled in the north gradually died down and the Latimers were content to live quietly with their neighbours as they had in times past.

Chapter 4 A Royal Encounter

   Lord Latimer also had a house in Chelsea which he had not visited for some months after the Pilgrimage of Grace but as time went by he decided to take Katherine up to London to visit the court. This sounded to Katharine infinitely more desirable than Snape Castle and she hoped that they would be made welcome despite the trouble with the Pilgrimage of Grace. Latimer was rather apprehensive also but decided that they could not remain away as social lepers to the King. She wondered which way they would be taking to London and queried the route with Latimer when they were sitting by the huge fire that evening.
'Why do you ask my love?' asked Latimer.
'We shall be going through the Midlands and I should love to see my friends the Throckmortons who live at Coughton Court not far from Warwick. Do you know of them?'
'I have heard the name and believe they are fellow Catholics who have kept their distance from court following their strong allegiance to the Pope. They may be a little unwise to visit at the moment but we shall not talk too much about the matter'.
'My cousin George Throckmorton has been in the Tower this many a day' said Katharine sadly.
'I will make some enquiries about the incident that caused his imprisonment and then decide if it's wise' he said.

It was over two weeks later when he received news from the Throckmortons who said that the punishment had not been on religious grounds but was a civil matter. They begged him to ask the King to release Sir George Throckmorton who had, it seemed, been incarcerated because of not paying dues to the King for some deer hunting lands which were crown property. They added that George had given the sum owing to Cromwell's office and that he had requested Cromwell to give it to the King. He had heard nothing of his expected release and had cautioned against employing Cromwell as a go-between. As his sin had not involved his Roman Catholic affiliations Latimer agreed to arrange to stay a night with them on the way down and would consider appealing to the King on his behalf if the occasion presented itself.

Katherine was delighted with his decision though somewhat apprehensive about the reception they would receive from the King, but as her husband seemed unconcerned she tried to ignore her fears. Never having travelled to London and of course, a stranger to the court, the future beckoned her as exciting and even thrilling. To her delight Lord Latimer who had previously been a frequent visitor to the court, received a personal invitation from the King to bring his new bride south to meet him. He obviously was not going to bear grudges and Latimer considered it politic to accept his invitation as soon as possible.

'So you see Katharine the King can be merciful if he so chooses and he is not going to make our lives miserable as he is well able to do. He has decided to bury old differences and we must be gracious in return and give him our loyalty and love. After all the Pilgrimage of Grace is in the past and times have moved on.'

Therefore he resolved to take his new young wife as soon as possible to introduce her to the King. 'Do not be afraid of King Henry' he advised. 'He is bluff and sometimes loud but at heart he is not so intimidating. His new Queen Anne, who was a Boleyn, will be there and he is deeply in love with her. Of course nobody mention Queen Katherine as she was known. She is not addressed as 'queen' even if her name unfortunately comes into the conversation. Be careful not to make Queen Anne jealous and be sure to listen carefully to what she says. On this, your first visit it will be wise to say little and observe much. In this way you will learn the manners of the court which are rather different from our usual life. People do not speak so readily and indeed not so bluntly as in the north, but they ponder deeply and have long memories'.

Lord Latimer brought in a seamstress to advise Katharine on the latest styles and to make some rich brocade dresses for her first visit to court. She chose golds and deep reds to tone with her auburn hair and when she tried on the dresses and saw the admiration in her husband's eyes she felt she had the confidence to meet the King without faltering, young as she was. She was very curious to see the King's new wife who had displaced her own mother's friend, despite feeling the sadness of the change.

The journey to London was long and wearisome, though seeing different parts of the country was intriguing and made up for the fleas in the beds. On one night they were glad to stay with the Throckmortons in the Midlands at Coughton Court and enjoyed the luxury of clean beds and water and friendly faces. Latimer was pleased to stay there and discussed the problems surrounding the Catholic Church when the servants had left. Coughton's owners were deeply Catholic still though they did not openly flaunt their religion. They had not seen Katharine since she was a youngster in the north. They admitted to sometimes housing Catholic priests from the continent for a time and they had the wherewithal necessary for Catholic services but not on show. 'After all the King remains an English catholic' they said 'but he does not favour any continental connection'.

They took them up to the tower on top of the hall from where they had someone on constant watch. So far they had been unmolested although living somewhat dangerously. They dwelt in hope that Catholics would be tolerated again if they were loyal to the King and did not flaunt their beliefs or their loyalty to the Pope.

That evening when supper was finished and cleared away discussion turned again to the sadness of Sir George Throckmorton being still in the Tower and the Throckmortons considered that they had discovered the reason for his continued imprisonment. They had thought much about Katherine's wish to try and have him released and hoped that Sir George might receive Henry's pardon if the Throckmortons sent the sum owing with the Latimers to the King. It could be misconstrued as a bribe which was a danger they were prepared to take but it should be mentioned as an old debt without incurring Cromwell's part in the matter. It was always better to keep on the right side of Cromwell even if he was in the wrong.

Katherine was comforted by this helpful thoughtfulness and tentatively suggested that the family should write to the King offering the money owed before they saw him. There was long discussion on the wisdom of this approach and when Katharine retired a decision still hung in the balance.

The next morning early they bade farewell to their kindly hosts and set out again on the final stages of their journey having promised to do what they could if possible for Sir George. The King had pardoned Latimer himself for the Pilgrimage of Grace and may be minded to do the same for his other relation. On the other hand the King might decide that a family repeatedly needing pardons was too much trouble to be borne.

Arriving at last in Chelsea was exciting and a great relief. The area was fascinating and novel to Katharine and London was magical to her with its fine timbered houses, its street cries, its elegant clothes and its darting young ruffians begging and cheekily grinning. It was so hectic and rowdy that it seemed a thousand miles away from the calmness of Snape Castle. She vowed to herself privately that if her husband gave her the choice of living in grim Snape Castle or in their Chelsea house she would plump for Chelsea every time. Notwithstanding that she was a northerner born and bred the south had gentler manners, climate and ambiance. She thought back to the time when she had first considered leaving the north and it had seemed to her like the end of her world. Her husband John seemed equally at home in either place and had a pleasant manner which made him welcome everywhere.

The size of Whitehall Palace was impressive and she now considered Snape Castle as not too large at all. 'Don't leave me my love' said Katharine. 'I might get lost in the maze of passages and never see you again'. Her husband smiled at her and said quietly 'You are a funny little thing. Take care you do not get gobbled up by a splendid being as a tasty morsel!'

Latimer seemed unfazed by the splendour of the King and his surroundings. He approached the King and spoke in low tones to him for what seemed to Katharine a long time after which the King nodded and waved an attendant to come closer to receive some orders.

When it came time for Katharine to meet the King she turned to her husband asking if anything was amiss with her dress. 'You look beautiful my love and I am sure the King will be beguiled. He is very fond of pretty women'. Katharine approached a little nearer to the thrones of the King and Queen and saw why people would find Henry intimidating. He was a huge bulk of a man, big enough to get three men inside his doublet some said. He looked boldly at Katharine and eyed her up and down with his beady eyes which missed nothing. He had a tiny mouth in an enormous square head and his watchful eyes flicked about as he spoke. Lord Latimer approached the throne again, squeezing Katherine's hand in reassurance. 'Your Majesty I would like to present to you my wife Katherine.' The King's small eyes raked her and he said slowly 'So it is Katherine is it?' The name of his first wife unfortunately resonated with him and a hostile expression crossed his face for a moment. Anne looked black. She gave Katharine a sharp look and then bowed her head saying nothing. 'Well, well my lady' said the King 'I wish you a goodly visit to Whitehall' and he gave her an appreciative stare. 'Is this your first visit to London?' Katharine would like to have nodded rather than speak but a little prod from her husband loosened her tongue.

'Indeed it is Your Majesty. I am honoured to visit my King and Queen' and as she said this made a sweeping curtsey. At this Katherine fancied she detected a faint smile from Queen Anne.

'Do you hunt or do you dance or do you do both things?' queried the King. Katharine smiled shyly and said that she would prefer to dance but she particularly liked to read.

'Well, well that is a novelty for a lady' said the King whilst Queen Anne seemed to lose interest in the conversation, or at least gave that impression. 'One day you shall tell me what you read'. Katherine trusted he would forget this as the thought of having a lengthy conversation with the King almost made her tremble. 'He is being courteous' she thought to herself.

In time Katherine became used to the King and being careful about what she said seemed to win his approval. With Queen Anne she never felt entirely comfortable and sensed that the Queen did not appreciate her husband holding conversations with other ladies. She was exceedingly beautiful with a small face and enormous, expressive brown eyes. The King was evidently besotted with her and she wore his admiration with jaunty pride. Katherine had heard it whispered that she was called in the London streets 'the goggle-eyed whore' but that fact she kept strictly to herself. After several audiences Katharine even plucked up courage in time to ask the King for a few words with him.

'Your Majesty' she said to him as she knelt before his throne. 'I have special thanks to make to you for the boon you have granted to my cousin as my husband tells me.' She looked up shyly at the King and he nodded his head. 'No more of that my lady – all is well. Some enquiries remain to be made into the length of his sentence and the reason for it being continued'. Henry stroked his chin and eyed Katharine speculatively. He was planning to remove Cromwell from power and perhaps even have him removed from this earth and he would welcome a chance to discomfort him.

'Well my Lady I hear your thanks. I will presently order that Sir George be released and he may present himself at court in due course'. Katharine was delighted at her own courage and the obliging nature of the King and thought back to the time when she was afraid even to speak to him. She recalled how she had trembled when she first met him. She kissed King Henry's hand in gratitude and he in turn gave her a long, appreciative stare. She could understand why women spoke of the King with reverence and even affection and reflected that power had its own magnetism.

Chapter 5   Windsor Ball

Lord Latimer was gratified by her success and proud of his young wife's ease of manner in what could have been an intimidating setting for a lady of less than thirty years unused to court circles.

'We will make a diplomat of you yet' he commented. 'I have something to impart which I rather think you will like' he said smiling and humming to himself.

'What is it, do tell me' said Katherine looking into his eyes and trying to guess his meaning.

'We are invited to attend a ball here that the King is holding tomorrow week'.

'How very ...exciting' breathed Katherine. 'But I am not used to dancing you know in public'.

'Fear not I have a friend who will teach you every day. He is a hunting servant actually but prides himself on his dancing. Will you learn in time do you think?'

'I will try my best indeed and I trust you will dance with me and tell me if I have learnt well'. So Katherine's time was taken up during the following week in learning the pavane and the galliard. She was warned that those two dances would be enough to learn at first and the lavolta she must be content to watch if it were to be danced at all as it was considered risqué. Katherine entered into the lessons with all the energy of youth and with a considerable grace and beauty of carriage. When her husband came to watch her the day before their court appearance he applauded her dexterity and gave his servant a purse which pleased him well.

The dance was to be held at Whitehall and Katherine was abrim with pleasure at her elegant new blue and silver dress in which she secretly hoped to be the belle of the ball or at least not to embarrass her husband. She tried the dress on to show him and paced the room slowly and elegantly before curtseying before him. Latimer raised her up and then asked her to curtsey to him as if he were the King. 'Smile briefly at the King and the Queen but do not hold their gaze long and wait for them to speak first if they wish to. Royal persons love quiet and respectful attention but of course they must initiate a conversation.' The evening of the dance came all too soon and Katharine tried to ignore the butterflies in her stomach. She thought that she could respond to the King but was very apprehensive of replying to Queen Anne. She was to learn in time that Queen Anne preferred speaking to gentlemen and that ladies were usually ignored.

There were liveried servants holding lights at the entrance to the palace and one of them detached himself and preceded them personally up into the great hall. Leading off from the main ballroom was a room with a long table covered with sweetmeats, grapes and glasses of sweet wine.

'No more than one glass of that my young wife' teased her husband. 'I doubt that you have tasted much wine before'. Katharine gave him a quizzical look. She was introduced to several friends of her lord's, some of whom she felt to be friendly and others who were dignified and said little. She was told that no dancing could begin until the King had appeared and danced with the Queen and Katherine waited expectantly for the fanfare which would herald their arrival. When the King and Queen entered she drew her breath in suddenly at the beauty of Queen Anne who proudly came in smiling to right and left and slightly leaning on the King's arm. She was dressed in gold brocade with a very low necked bodice and with a matching head-dress of pearls and gold flowers. The King looked very proud of her as she flashed her beautiful large eyes at her admirers who clustered to see her captivating appearance. The King led the Queen onto the floor in an elegant pavanne which was a slow, processional dance in which she could show herself off to advantage. When they had circled the room the other dancers joined in behind them and Lord and Lady Latimer trod the floor slowly looking into each other's eyes. As the dance came to a close Lord Latimer leaned over to Katherine and whispered 'well done Katherine. You are a quick learner'. Katherine was delighted that she had performed well and was content to watch proceedings taking in the beauty of the silk dresses glowing in the candlelight.

'Now is your test with the galliard' said Lord Latimer as he took Katherine back onto the dance floor and waited for the beating music to begin. This dance was more testing and Katherine drew a deep breath and prepared for the challenge. The King and Queen did not join in this energetic dance but watched from their dais with interest. The music struck up and the handsome couple paced off with the other dancers preparing for the last two beats when Katherine would be lifted high to land with softness and elegance as she had been taught. All went well and after circling the floor twice Lord Latimer drew Katherine out and spoke quietly to her telling her to watch the Queen who had left the King after whispering in his ear. She was partnered by a young nobleman who was obviously dazzled by her appearance and his task. She gazed into his eyes as she landed and Katherine glanced at the King who was watching her keenly with an expression which made Katherine afraid of him. It was a mixture of keen interest with not a little jealousy and Katherine was glad that she was not his wedded wife.

Katherine was introduced to several lords and ladies whose names she hoped to remember and she conducted herself with grace and dignity aware that she was causing some interest amongst those courtiers who had not seen her dancing before. The evening passed all too quickly and when the King led his Queen out of the room, turning round to bow to their guests, the couples began to drift away knowing that this was their cue to bring the evening to an end. It had been both exciting and daunting for Katherine but she knew that she had carried herself well and that her husband had been proud of her.

Chapter 6 Enter Seymour

As Katherine became more familiar with the court she drew to herself other ladies of similar age with some more open to the new fresh air of religious practices though she was always guarded in speaking out. She also found that she had unwittingly attracted the attention of a good looking gentleman who, she was told, was of the Seymour family and who had a sister Jane who sometimes came to court and was both graceful and attractive. When she glanced round she would sometimes see Seymour willing her to smile at him. Lord Latimer thought Thomas Seymour was somewhat shallow and flirtatious but he had to admit that he was popular with the ladies of the court. More seriously he considered him very ambitious to have influence at court and that he should be treated with caution.
'In my opinion' he said 'the Seymours are nothing if not power seeking and are eager to work their way into authority at court'.
'What sort of power?' asked Katharine. 'Any sort of power that will bring them closer to the throne. Thomas Seymour may look a pleasant, unassuming sort of man but he is no less ambitious than the rest'. Katharine mulled this over to herself and was at a loss to think how such a pleasant and apparently light hearted man could hope to further his career under Henry's watchful eyes. However she was new to court intrigue and had little doubt that her husband had the measure of the Seymours by some means or other.
'For all I know Thomas Seymour may be merely pleasant and unassuming but I doubt it' he added. 'It will be interesting to watch his progress'.

Over the next few months Katharine and Lord Latimer became frequent visitors to Chelsea and the court when it was in Whitehall or Hampton Court and on one occasion they were asked to stay for dinner. A messenger had approached Lord Latimer with the invitation. It was not a novelty for him as he had dined with the King on more than one occasion. But to Katharine it was an unnerving thought to have to make conversation to such a mighty and capricious personage. Although this was a signal honour and to be seated at the end of the King's table was a mark of esteem, Katherine was apprehensive about eating the correct thing in the right way. The King she noticed ate ravenously as though he had not eaten all day and he certainly didn't pay any attention to his table manners. If someone close to the King addressed a remark to him, he did not stop eating, neither did he look at his interlocutor, but made his reply whilst still looking at his plate. Katherine reflected that her mother would have had something to say about such churlish and greedy manners. She also privately thought that with his bulk he would surely benefit from eating less. If he continued in this fashion he would be as broad as long! She was much relieved to find that she was seated just far enough away from the King to make it impossible to carry on a conversation with him. Once when she was watching him covertly he caught her eye and winked at her. She felt her neck and face turning bright red or so it seemed and she was wary of watching him again. The ladies who were seated close to her ate sparingly and were careful not to let their silks become besmirched with grease. They came into their own with the sweetmeats which they could nibble with some elegance whilst preserving their appearance. Katherine tasted for the first time a delicious syllabub made, she was informed, with cream and honey and a spice she could not identify. She half smiled when she thought what her dear departed mother would have said about the King's lack of finesse at the table and she steered her eyes away from him apart from a quick glance when he was talking to his neighbour. After the banquet Latimer spoke quietly to Katharine and asked her what she had thought of the feast. 'It was very splendid' she replied 'but I had to be careful not to soil my silk dress. I was astonished by the King's appetite. The Queen hardly seems to eat at all but just picks and nibbles. And can you guess what the King did?'

'Well, what did he do apart from not eating you?'

'He winked at me!'

'My goodness how daring! Perhaps he feels he would like to wed you' he laughed. Katharine thought he had the fascination of a lion like the one she had seen at the Tower. He was both dangerous and appealing in a strange sort of way. His bold stare at her had been oddly exciting and challenging at the same time.

The King was known to favour the new English religion which leaned towards Protestantism as a result of his long disputes with Rome and the Pope. However he never considered himself a Protestant and all his life was in his own eyes, an English Catholic. He considered the new religion as very much his own - perhaps Catholicism without Rome with a touch of Protestantism without Luther as opposed to a religion which had provoked and angered him during his lengthy divorce from his first queen Katherine of Aragon. His was the new style of Catholicism with himself as the head of the church and not the Pope. Anyone caught practising old style Catholicism would put his life and living in an invidious position. Treading carefully was the watchword in a time of flux.

Although Lord Latimer had taken part in the Pilgrimage of Grace which was a protest against the sequestration of the wealth of the Catholic monasteries, the extent of Henry's favour was shown by his seeming to forget his involvement much to Katharine's relief. Katherine was grateful and puzzled by his convenient forgetfulness and queried this with her lord. 'We are indeed fortunate that the King does not hold the recent protest against you and or even worse imprison you' she said. 'The King is not a vindictive man' he replied when they were alone and private. 'He either takes immediate revenge or seems to forget the trouble altogether. With myself it was fortunately the latter'.

She reflected that some had parted company with their heads for less than that. He was fortunate indeed that Henry chose to overlook his leanings which in others often led to disgrace or death. Katharine wisely kept her new style Protestant sympathies to herself and avoided embarrassing her husband and alienating her King. For anyone who attended court, religion was a tightrope to walk and fixed views could lead to deep trouble. 'Listen well and speak little' was the mantra of wise courtiers when the subject of religion reared its dangerous head.

Over the years she witnessed the demise of Henry's wives and the unspoken horror of their fates. Walls had ears and it was best to accept the King's actions without overt comment. Anne Boleyn, the proud beauty she had first met was beheaded for infidelity though perhaps if she had produced a son and heir it might have been different. That she had produced a daughter was not considered a gift of the first order. Katharine had heard that she had requested a French executioner to end her brief life with a sword rather than an axe. This only prolonged her agonised wait for death as the executioner was held up in his travels and twice her death was postponed. Katharine shuddered to think what Anne's little daughter Elizabeth would make of her father who had had her mother executed. Although she had never become close to the Queen she nevertheless felt sickened to think of that proud beauty kneeling on Tower Green to face her brutal death. Any woman who consents to be the King's consort must be mad, she thought!

In what seemed a very little time Henry had taken to himself a new Queen called Jane Seymour, the sister of the Thomas whom Katherine had briefly met. She seemed a demure and pious lady who took life very seriously and was quite different from her brother. However there were those who thought Jane was steel beneath the apparently retiring appearance and that her elevation was cleverly planned. Although Katherine never had a conversation with the new Queen she observed her from a distance and thought her rather solemn and prim. However Henry was apparently besotted with her and she sealed his admiration by giving him the male heir he had longed for so long. Sadly this Queen did not last long after the birth and Katherine never saw her again. Childbirth was a dangerous affair in those days and Jane succumbed to its fevers and infections. Although she had steered clear of the gallows, childbed had proved equally dangerous. Henry fled from her deathly presence and her demise spread gloom throughout the court. For a time courtiers thought that the King would not want to marry again. Henry was genuinely heartbroken by Jane's death and ordered her burial at Windsor where he planned to lie beside her when his time was come. His wish to be eventually buried with her was fulfilled, but his desire for a great carved statue of himself and Jane never materialized.

Jane's brother Thomas Katharine had met and he had shown particular interest in her. She sensed he was very ambitious and would try to have close relations with the new Seymour baby prince, the apple of the King's eye. The King himself was less enamoured of Jane's brother and probably found his attitude to the ladies irritating.

However, Henry had not finished with marriage and the subsequent wedding to Anne of Cleves followed by an amicable divorce caused some to say that Holbein might be the one to guard his neck for painting a too flattering portrait of her for Henry's approval when he selected her unseen. There were those who quietly whispered that she was a German mare following her predecessor the English purebred. Katherine had not been enamoured of the German Queen and had reason to dislike her acerbic tongue when she herself was wed to Henry. After Anne Boleyn and the beloved Jane Seymour Anne certainly seemed to have missed the good fairy when looks were handed out. Lady Latimer met Anne once when visiting the court and she considered her not only plain with a long nose but also rather lacking in manners. When Katherine spoke to her she received a haughty look from Anne which after a lengthy silence produced the terse remark. 'I do not understand'. On this Anne walked away and took no further interest in Katherine. Anne however, had no intention of returning home after her divorce and enjoyed the advantages of a good life with no demands on her person or her purse. Henry tolerated her continual presence rather than aggravating her German relatives by dispatching her back to Cleves. It may be thought that Anne of Cleves's unattractiveness saved her life in a way that the beauty of others led them astray and down the fatal path of execution. Henry had decided that instead of a normal divorce from Anne, she would be known as his sister so that no feathers would be ruffled on the continent. One bold courtier whispered that he would not even have chosen a horse himself unseen. Fortunately the remark never reached Henry's ears. Anne fared handsomely in her divorce settlement and was given several beautiful houses as well as a privileged position at the English court.

Finally came the execution of Katherine Howard for pre-marital sexual exploits and Katharine Latimer was not alone in pitying any lady whose beauty caught the King's eye and especially one whose tarnished reputation caught up with her. It was as well for Queen Katherine Howard that she did not have a child to leave behind her on earth though it caused unspoken horror to know the fate of this young beauty. It was whispered that she had been very close to the Princess Elizabeth who was deeply affected by her death. The Princess wept copiously that her young and gay companion suffered the ultimate punishment.

'How can it be that whoever I like and love is snatched away from me?' she sobbed. However, If Henry proposed marriage to someone of his choice she would be a foolhardy woman to refuse him. Katharine had heard that the Princess Elizabeth had been deeply shocked by the death of Katharine Howard and had vowed never to marry herself.

Frequent marriages had not improved Henry's temper and he was noticed to be often irritable and short with people. Katherine rather thought that his winking at ladies might have been dropped from his catalogue of attention to them. Unfortunately he found it hard to resist attainable beauties. In

Katherine Howard's case it was how she had behaved before her marriage that had sealed her fate.

Henry's self indulgent eating had told on his now corpulent body and he had developed a noticeable limp from an ulcerated leg caused by a jousting accident in his youth. Lady Latimer reflected that he was probably unlikely to do any further jousting as well as winking nowadays.

It was about this time that Lord Latimer became indisposed with an undiagnosed illness and he was often absent from court. The doctors, with their limited knowledge were baffled.

'Lady Latimer we must hope for the best and you must give your husband eggs in milk and no meat for the most part. Lord Latimer is a strong man and will take time to be cured. Meanwhile keep the windows closed and keep his brow cool.'

Katharine once again found herself in the position of nurse to a sick husband. She summoned another doctor who bled him copiously and suggested a possible problem of the liver. However diagnosis was of a primitive kind at this stage and was a tentative suggestion on the whole. Latimer took to his bed and became weaker daily before Katharine's anxious eyes. She preferred to nurse her husband herself rather than have him further debilitated by bloodletting or leeches. It was never known irrefutably what Lord Latimer's sickness was caused by but all the leeches and potions of the medical men failed to restore him to full health. Katherine felt sick at heart when she considered that perhaps again she was to lose her husband whose company and activities she so much enjoyed. She devoted herself to his care when he became sick and their visits to court became fewer and fewer.

He took comfort from praying with Katharine rather than visits from the priest and often fell asleep during their devotions.

During their last visit to court before Lord Latimer took to his bed, the King had taken the trouble to commiserate with Lord Latimer and to recommend his own medical man. But in those days medical knowledge was sparse and if leeches did not avail it was hard to know where to turn for worthwhile advice. If the King's doctors could not cure his suppurating leg how could they be of help to her husband?

In these deeply upsetting circumstances Katharine was taken aback to be sent presents from the King consisting of costly gowns and sleeves which were usually attached separately. They were embroidered with gold thread and seed pearls and made Katharine gasp with pleasure combined with shock when she unwrapped them. Although her husband was ill she felt obliged to ask his advice on the embarrassing situation she found herself in.

'My dear lord, what am I to do about these gifts from the King which I find most unwelcome at any time but especially now? Should I thank him or try to ignore them as proceeding from some error?' Lord Latimer's illness had worsened and he spoke quietly to Katharine as she sat by his bedside.

'My dear wife, you have been a faithful and devoted spouse and you have pleased the King with your pious discussions and learned interventions whilst never compromising the sacred bonds of marriage. After my death......no, no do not protest for I feel the end is in sight, you must choose what is the wisest and best course for yourself. If the King should decide on you as his next wife you have my blessing but never forget the unfortunate deaths of his unwise queens. Be always vigilant never to give fuel to the flames of your enemies, for such people are always present. You have my blessing in whatever you do'.

Katherine was beside herself with grief at the thought of losing her dearly loved husband who was so detached about what seemed to be his approaching end. She summoned the priest to visit him and pray with him and he seemed to take comfort from that. Sometimes he would wake up with a cry 'Where am I?' or 'Stay near me' and Katharine would sit holding his hand, trying to disguise her tears.

Once he called Katharine to listen to him which was difficult as his voice was low and fading. 'I know the sadness of losing a loved one and so do you. I fear for your life with the King if that is what is to be.' He paused for a while whilst he recovered his breath. He repeated his previous warnings which obviously preoccupied him.

Fearing for Katharine's life with the King might have included the infidelities which Henry's previous wives had had to endure. These included amongst the known ones Lady Elizabeth Fitzwilliam, Elizabeth Blount, Mary Boleyn, Anne's own sister and Madge Shelton.

But Latimer was not thinking about these extra marital affairs, if indeed he knew of them. He was thinking more of the legal wives who had come to unfortunate ends.

'You know as well as I do the fates of the King's previous wives and I tremble to think what may happen to you if you incur his wrath. Be always vigilant of enemies who will be jealous and always follow the King's wishes in religion as in everything. His beliefs are somewhat different from my own in that he does not hold the Pope in awe. But beware of traps set by others and................' with this he tailed off and closed his eyes.

Sighing deeply he fell into a restless sleep. Katharine knew that her husband would want a Catholic burial with Catholic rites and rituals and trusted that the King would not be offended by that if, indeed, he found out. She decided to leave the arrangements for his funeral in the hands of their priest who would administer the last rites. If she had had a free rein to order the service she would have preferred a less avowedly Catholic one but that would have caused controversy locally if not further afield. However her husband's wishes must take precedence. The thoughts of her future as a widow she could not dismiss from her mind and this made her quail sometimes. Katharine held John's hand whilst the slow tears fell on the coverlet. If the King was really weighing her up as a future bride she could not turn away from it, but rather than embracing her apparent royal destiny she felt the weight of unwelcome responsibility on her shoulders. To herself she considered that the King's attentions at this time showed a lack of tact and sensitivity though some would find them flattering above all.

   She loved her husband and she knew the generosity of his love in giving his blessing to her possibly unwelcome future and realised there was no turning away. She was still only thirty one years of age and an attractive woman though having endured the sorrow of being widowed twice. In Latimer's will he left two manor houses to Katharine and a considerable fortune despite the monies he had paid to Cromwell to escape from jail.

Katherine was left a wealthy widow though a desperately sorrowing one and no doubt a target for possible fortune hunters.

   She received many messages of sorrow from neighbours and friends at court, among them a message of condolence from Thomas Seymour.

She had the sad task of arranging her late husband's funeral at old St Paul's in London. She would have preferred a quiet ceremony at their local church but his standing at court demanded a more prestigious ceremony and burial which would befit his noble rank. It was an ordeal especially daunting for a young widow and Katherine, although not present at the service as women were not permitted, resolved to visit his grave privately in the future to say her farewell alone. She planned to be buried beside him if she remained a widow, but that was never to be as Fate would dictate and actually Latimer's grave was lost the following century during the Great Fire of London.

Chapter 7 Regina's Family

When Lord Latimer died Katharine faced the predicament of being alone and wealthy and wondering how to continue her life when her period of mourning came to an end. She knew well that the King has been putting his mark on her by sending her gifts when she was not yet widowed. If she ignored these and accepted another offer she would put her future in jeopardy. She contemplated what life would be like if she were brave enough to marry the King if he should actually propose to her.

Two of his wives had ended up on the scaffold at Tower Green and she shuddered to think of the mental and physical torture of their fates. One was divorced and virtually banished to lead a life of regret and loneliness far from her homeland. One had died in childbirth and was still idolised apparently by the King. The only one who had come out well of her marriage was the ill favoured and ill mannered Anne of Cleves who had ended up as Henry's 'sister' and escaped lightly. None of the alternatives presented a pleasant and inviting future and besides she might possibly have her own ideas about a suitable husband if she must have one and there was no doubt life with a husband could be easier and safer.

One such offer was not slow in coming and that was from the brother of the late Queen Jane Seymour. Thomas, a man five years her senior was the first man to show an interest in Katharine who was not somewhat older than her. He had been attentive to Katherine and to other ladies at court where his ready wit and charm had often amused her. Now that she was again unmarried she was at liberty to spend more time with this lively adventurer when her period of mourning should be over, without attracting adverse comments apart from the danger of those from the King. It appeared to some at court that the comely widow might be contemplating marriage for the third time as Seymour did not hide his interest in her.

He seemed to come from nowhere one day and appeared behind her.
'Well my lady, what are you thinking I wonder? Dare I ask you to share your thoughts with me?'
'I have many things to think about and many memories to recall'.
'Indeed we all have my lady but we must not let regrets from the past stand in the way of happiness for the future'.
Katherine smiled a little but said nothing. She was aware of being covertly watched by onlookers.
'I know you like dancing for I saw you at the King's ball at Whitehall last year and a fine dancer you are. You need someone to teach you other dances perhaps? Would you honour me by being my partner next time you are invited to a dance?'
'I doubt whether I shall dance again as the memories are too bitter-sweet.'
'Nay do not say 'never'. Whilst you are still young my lady life is to be lived'. Katharine smiled a little sadly at him and giving him

a low curtsey she made her way out of the gallery before Sir Thomas Seymour could say more.

However an unfortunate family incident occurred before long which took precedence over everything else. Katherine's brother William who was now also at court accused his wife of adultery and followed the King's example by pressing for the death penalty to be imposed on her.

Katherine was deeply shocked by his intention and determined to change his plan of action. Thinking back to their childhood Katharine recalled William watching a wounded rabbit dying without giving it a merciful release and knew there was a streak of cruelty in his make-up. She was appalled by this turn of events and tried with all her powers of persuasion, to turn her brother away from this course of action.

'My dear William I beg you to think carefully before taking such drastic action. Because there are some in higher places who hold such action to be appropriate, remember that we are only people of humble origins who do not take such actions as those. Blessed are the merciful I say and I believe. Please, please listen to your sister'.

'Humble indeed – what nonsense you do talk. I think your mind has been upset by your tragic experience. We are not so humble, as our Mother was close to Queen Katharine of Aragon'.

'Hush William, do not mention that name so freely.
If word reached the King it might be the worse for us and may be in serious trouble.'

He would not listen and stormed that he had been made to a fool and a cuckold. 'What did the King do when he found his wife philandering with other men?' he demanded.

'But your wife is a good lady and would not behave in such a manner' she said. 'And what about the children?' she added.

'They would live under a cloud for the remainder of their lives. Anyway you have no absolute proof. You know what gossip is like at the court'. Katharine protested that he had no evidence and was depending on rumours and putting his good wife's life in jeopardy on hearsay. William was disinclined to listen to Katharine and stumped off in a temper. In desperation Katharine took the matter straight to the King who stroked his chin whilst eyeing Katharine closely and said that he was unable to intervene unless her husband pardoned his wife. Katherine boldly replied 'Your Majesty is above the law and I will try to get my brother to pardon her'.

Katherine took William to one side where they would not be overheard.

'William' she said 'I am so upset that you doubt your dear wife's loyalty without having any certain proof either way. She has sworn her fidelity to you on the Bible. What else can she do? Do not rush into demanding her death. Perhaps those who say she has deceived you are lying. Would you rather believe them than your wife? I am not a brutal woman but I would rather you had the witnesses put to torture than just accepted their word.' William turned away pensively and then turned back to glare at Katharine.

'What would you think about this I ask you? I found a diamond brooch in her treasure box and it was not one that I gave her. More than that however, I found them talking together in earnest not knowing that I was nearby and I also found a letter from him to her. When he saw me he made off with a quick bow and said nothing. The King would not and did not tolerate such things from his Queens and no more do I. People are laughing about me behind my back.'

'What does your wife say when you ask her about these things?' asked Katherine.

'She denies them of course. What else would she do? However I have had my closest friend watch out for her and he confirms my suspicions. She is making a fool of me before the court. She must go and that is that!' Before he could speak again she said quietly 'I have spoken to His Majesty and he said that if you would forgive her he would spare her'. William looked searchingly at her. 'Such influence you have nowadays!' Katharine said nothing but leaned forward and kissed him on the cheek. William gave her a rueful half smile and said 'for your sake sister I will not insist her life is taken but she will have a price to pay'. Katharine smiled her joy and hugged William.

'Mother would have been proud of you' she said. William had begrudgingly capitulated and his wife was spared though forced to give her estates over to her husband and to see her children declared bastards. Katharine was deeply shocked by William's actions and would have argued forcefully with him if he had been prepared to listen.

The King was sympathetic to Katharine to some extent but Katharine appreciated that his own experiences hardly encouraged him to doubt a wife's possible infidelity. Perhaps to impress Katharine Henry made William Earl of Essex. He was subsequently admitted to serve on the Privy Council and made a Knight of the Garter. Surprised and amazed by these promotions William sought Katharine out. 'Why have I been so honoured thus by the King? Have you had a hand in this? You seem to have the King's ear!' Katharine was unable to say why William had been so honoured though at the back of her mind she could make a guess. Henry was known to favour the relatives of women he wanted to know better.

Katharine's heart quailed within her as she realised what lay behind Henry's actions but was unable to say anything about it. However unless and until Henry made an overt move towards her she followed her own heart for the first time though was careful to act with discretion.

When she was in the same room as the King she could sense without looking that he kept glancing at her. She pondered on the possibility of returning to the north of England to her old home ground. But she knew that the King would track her down if he wanted her and then she would have to explain herself which would be uncomfortable to say the least. Besides she would be a lone target for fortune hunters as a wealthy widow. William's rapid elevations did not prevent Katharine's continued attachment to Seymour which perhaps unintentionally provoked the King. Although she was circumspect in the extreme when she was talking to Seymour she did not know who, if anyone, was spying on her and perhaps inventing stories to curry favour with the King. She suspected Seymour was an adventurer who would pursue what he saw as the main chance, but nevertheless she found his undoubted charm and teasing irresistible. The more she saw of him the more she realised that she was falling under his spell and the more she longed to be wedded to him and away from the perils of court life. His teasing light heartedness gave a lift to her spirits as no one had before.

Seymour was a dapper, lean and handsome man with a pleasant manner and a lively sense of humour and was an undoubted favourite with the ladies. He had light golden hair and pointed beard and a merry eye and ready laugh. He took great care with his appearance and wore fashionable clothes which became his lithe figure. In fact she rather thought he prided himself on being a dandy. Being slim he carried his apparel with grace and distinction whereas the King with his unwholesome bulk could look magnificent but was ever gross. Katharine could hardly think that Thomas and the prim and dignified Queen Jane Seymour had been brother and sister.

Seymour was also extremely ambitious as regards his possible influence over his young nephew the future King. He felt somewhat aggrieved that he, the uncle of the future King was denied free access to him. After all he was more part of the regal family than anyone living. Katharine put that to the back of her mind but more urgently was uncertain if he was a womaniser or just good company. He had a way of appearing behind her and startling her by putting his hands around her waist, blowing on the nape of her neck and then laughing and stroking his golden beard. Henry knew about Seymour's behaviour or was told about it. Whichever it was it gnawed into his mind until the day he died. In fact when he lay dying it was suggested to him that Seymour might be on the Council and dying as he was then he summoned the strength to shout 'No, no, no!'

However at this time Thomas Seymour's charms worked on Katharine if not on Henry. He stole up behind her and touched her shoulder.

'What are you planning today my fair lady?' he would say as he smiled quizzically at her. 'Will you favour me and walk in the gardens or have you some serious business to attend to?' She could tell he was laughing at her and considered that although he rather took liberties in his addresses to her, his pleasant and playful manner was exceptionally winning. Both of her previous husbands had been men of more serious disposition and certainly not flirtatious.

She had discussed her favourite subject, religion, with both of her previous husbands and especially Lord Latimer had been happy to spend time on that topic. With Sir Thomas religion was not the subject closest to his heart. In fact she rather doubted that he was religious at all in the normal sense of the word. He seemed devoted to the delicious pleasures of 'now'. All her instincts told her not to trust him as she feared that he was too much of a ladies' man. However she was intrigued to know what his relations had been and were with other ladies in the court, but she realized it was indiscreet to enquire. She just kept her eyes and ears open and was vigilant.

Meanwhile and more pressing was the attention of the King. He was not accustomed to being blocked in his desires. He may have considered that he had made his wishes perfectly clear by the gifts he had sent to Katharine and that she should be aware of that and give him her full attention. In his youth he had been dashing and handsome and in his own mind he was still that man and King to boot.

'Well my lady' he said one day when she had been talking to him about a little book of religious meditations which she much admired. 'When are you going to wear the sleeves which I sent you? I would like to see how they look on you and how they match your colouring. Perhaps you do not like them?'

'Indeed Sire I wrote you my warmest thanks for your kind gift which I will wear next time I come to court. They seemed too precious to me to actually wear but I will obey Your Majesty's wishes'. He had a way of watching her closely in company which she was aware of although she tried not to show it. She was especially conscious of his eyes on her when Seymour came to speak to her. Perhaps he was jealous of his dashing youth and thought back to the days when he was the dynamic and handsome idol of the court, unbeatable at jousting and tireless at dancing in the evenings; in the days before he had injured his leg in a riding accident. In those days he had not had a lame and suppurating leg to tax his temper. Nothing daunted however, Henry seemed determined to marry Katharine and took matters into his own hands. He called Seymour to his presence

'I have an honour to bestow on you Sir Thomas and it is one for which you are eminently suited. I am making you the ambassador to the court of the Regent of the Netherlands. You will remain there and report back to me by courier. The post is permanent'. With sinking heart Seymour replied 'I thank Your Majesty for your generous appointment and I will fulfil it to the height of my ability. I will always represent Your Majesty faithfully and dutifully and report back to Your Majesty regularly'.

Katherine was mortified by the unwelcome promotion of her suitor and her growing affection came to the fore at last. She bade him a tender farewell although she said nothing of stronger feelings. She felt the net closing around her. 'It would seem that His Majesty is removing you from the court because he intends to marry yet again and I begin to fear that I am to be his future wife.' What the King wanted the King obtained, if not by voluntary means then by force. The thought of the burden of marriage to the King who had removed so many wives appalled Katharine, but she knew she had no choice. She wrote to Seymour later. 'As truly as God is God, my mind was fully bent the other time I was at liberty to marry you before any man I know.' So at last he knew the depth of her feelings for him and smiled to himself. She was not going to the first woman to resist his charms!

Katherine was obliged to hide her true leanings and to appear to welcome the King's advances though in her heart longing to be free. In appearance he was far from desirable being 'so fat that such a man had never been seen. Three of the biggest men that could be found could get inside his doublet'. So wrote the author of the Spanish Chronicle and other eyewitnesses have confirmed his repellent appearance. He also had the infected leg, the result of a youthful jousting accident, which smelled unpleasant when dressed and did not improve his unpredictable humour. Yet ever blind to his own drawbacks he had considered Anne of Cleves to be malodorous as well as fat when he bedded her though he had declared that he was not attracted to closer physical contact.

A man who had sent two wives to their ghastly deaths was not an attractive proposition as a bridegroom, but nothing daunted Henry who was accustomed to getting his own way. He seemed to Katharine to be unaware of his unappealing appearance as he turned his thoughts to love songs and cast admiring looks at her. If his attentions had been to some other woman she would have relished the absurdity of the situation but as she herself was involved, the comedy was considerably lessened. She also had the unpleasant feeling that some of the courtiers were watching the action play out to their carefully concealed amusement. She humoured him as best she could whilst fearing that she was trying to train a dragon not to devour her. Fate had dealt her a hand she could not deny and she turned her back on love and faced her destiny with all the courage she could muster. She reflected that she had been fortunate to have had two happy marriages which was more than most women.

As long as Henry did not mention matrimony Katharine felt relatively safe but one day he inevitably did propose marriage to her. He had asked her to come with him into the garden at Windsor and they sat on a bench together enjoying the flowers and the sunshine.

'You look pensive and rather lonely nowadays my lady' he said to her leaning over to her and kissing her hand. 'I could make you the happiest of ladies and you would want for nothing. What do you say my dear lady? I have waited for you long enough Katharine' he said, turning to face her and taking her hand which he again kissed fervently. 'When are you going to be my helpmeet and Queen?' He was like an eager schoolboy somehow in his pleading but she knew he was serious and would brook no refusal.

'I am deeply honoured Your Majesty' she said. 'I will indeed be your Queen and wife and will seek always to please you'. He kissed her hand passionately and looked as happy as she had ever seen him. She put her fears to one side and determined to do her best in the role that Fate had decreed for her. Yet within her breast she knew that her heart belonged to Seymour, philanderer or no.

Katherine was used to sometimes demanding marriages with rather older men and, with her love of children, used to winning the affection of stepchildren. Henry was nearly thirty years older than she was and had an unpredictable temper. Katherine's calm and equable disposition would be a great asset in challenging circumstances. It would take all her powers of tact and diplomacy to weather this royal and repugnant coupling. However he had three children whose presence Katharine would much like to enjoy. After one of her discussions with the King she carefully broached the subject.

'Your Majesty, how I long to know your children and to have them at court. They would surely be a joy to Your Majesty and be grateful for your guidance in their learning. For my own part I so look forward to meeting the young prince and the two princesses'. The King stroked his beard and drummed his fingers on the table.

'We will see Katharine, we will see. Prince Edward does not need the distractions of court at his young age. There will be time for that when he is done with book learning. I dare say the two princesses would be company for you in time, but let us not hurry events'. Katharine knew better than to pursue her wishes but lost no opportunity of enquiring after their health and schooling when they spoke together. Her love of learning and her active mind would be a quality which had mostly eluded his previous wives, though to be overly enquiring certainly in religious matters could be a fraught and even dangerous trait. She was an intelligent conversationalist and could distract Henry from the nagging pain of his leg. Sometimes she would engage him in discussions about religious rites and beliefs.

'What are your views on salvation Your Majesty? Do you think mercy is granted through prayer to God or through the power of the priest?'

Henry drummed his fingers of the arm of the chair and looked hard at her. 'It is not for individuals to divine the limits of their rights' he said rather testily. 'The priest must direct the congregation in those matters. However the Pope has no say in matters in the English church'.

Although she also loved to discourse religion with Cranmer and to pick his brains she was careful not to commit herself to the side of the new Protestantism where her sympathies increasingly lay. She was always aware that her thoughts might be relayed to the King to her disadvantage. Cramner was a churchman she much respected but who knew what he might say to the King under pressure. She was not reluctant however, to express her aversion to the Pope, an opinion which was at one with Cranmer and the King. She wrote of him 'He was and is the greater persecutor of all true Christians than ever was Pharaoh of the children of Israel'. This view endeared her to the King but when she went further on occasion he had reason to ask himself who was the Head of the English church - himself or his wife?

However in her own composition entitled 'The Lamentations of a Sinner' she advocated obedience to husbands and 'silence in the congregation,' a precept which won royal approval but which to her cost she was later unable to follow. At the time it impressed Henry who was intrigued to find a potential bride with intellectual leanings coupled with a modest demeanour. But he did not approve of her assuming too much in the way of individual religious decision. That would be the beginning of the end for royal prerogative if it were carried through. He would ask her sometimes 'Who is the head of the English church?' and she would reply dutifully 'Your Majesty without any doubt is the head of our church in England'.

'What position do the priests have then? Are they above their King, below him or his equal?'

'Your Majesty is the head indeed' she would reply.

'Then who is the intercessor with God, the King or the priest?'

'Your Majesty by the grace of God knows the answer to this question' she replied tentatively.

'Would Cramner agree with you?'

'It is for Your Majesty to answer questions which are too difficult for a mere woman' came the response which satisfied him.

However there were those who looked with a jealous eye on her literary and religious aspirations as they saw them and who would fan the flames of Henry's jealousy. This was not difficult for he was ever on guard for anyone, even a potential wife, abrogating his own rights as Supreme Head of the Church of England. Whatever her religious aspirations her pleasant and open personality made her a general favourite and a welcome change from the coquetry of some of Henry's previous choices.

It could be that Katharine, in trying to find conversational subjects to distract the King from his painful leg, chose religion as the subject of interest to them both but one that Henry regarded as his sole area of authority.

In 1543 Henry and Katharine were married in the ornate Hampton Court chapel with its breathtaking ceiling. They spoke their vows in the presence of an ex wife, Lady Anne of Cleves who had made herself very much at home in the English court and was no doubt relieved to be a witness rather than a participant. She later commented acidly 'A fine burden Madam Katharine has taken on herself' perhaps recalling with some jealousy the times Henry had turned away from her in bed as being overweight and unwashed. The Lord Chancellor Wriothesley more generously wrote that Henry had 'never had a wife more agreeable to his heart'. His initial admiration would in time be qualified in a way which nearly brought both Katherine and himself down, but at that moment he was all in favour of the new Queen. He had a neat way of reflecting the King's own thoughts which was often the way to find favour.

Thomas Seymour, banished to the Netherlands would have been discomforted to know that Katharine had written to others to say that marriage to Henry 'was the greatest comfort that could happen to me'. It may be that this felicity was not assumed and it was certainly tactful. Henry thought the same as he made the marriage vows for the sixth time with great joy on his face and all seemed to bode well for a happy period.

Henry was content to remain at Hampton Court whilst Katharine organised the members of her household including her stepdaughter from Gainsborough days, Lady Agnes Tyrwhitt who was to be one of her ladies.

Agnes was overjoyed to be invited to court by Katharine and they spent many a happy hour reminiscing on former times in Gainsborough Old Hall. Katherine could not hear enough of the boys and was always interested in their lives and occupations. They put their heads together and happily passed the time going over their past amusements in Norfolk.

'My sons missed you when you left us' said Agnes, 'and the tutor also sang your praises, encouraging them in their studies. The boys used to tell me stories of how you explored the woods on the estate with them and how you and they used to rather tease Giant the bull'. They happily reminisced and laughed like schoolgirls and Katherine blessed the day that she had asked Agnes to be a part of her entourage.

Henry meanwhile had devised an unusual surprise for Katherine in the form of a test; the idea having been given to him by Bishop Gardiner who was not averse to fomenting trouble. He called his new wife to his side to acquaint her with his plans for the celebration he had in store.

'My dear wife, I am glad to be able to apprise you of an unusual surprise which I have devised to please you. I have determined that we shall now move the court back to Windsor.

To celebrate our wedding I have ordered that three Protestant heretics shall be burnt to death in Windsor Great Park'. He looked at her closely to ascertain her reaction for he had heard that she was perhaps closer to the reforming Cranmer than was wise. Katharine showed her steel then for she did not blench but replied carefully 'such is the fate of those who follow too closely the Lutheran precepts'. It may be thought nowadays from the safety of centuries that Katharine was duplicitous but in truth she had no alternative. Henry was satisfied by her response despite his former doubts about the extent of her espousal of the new credos. Marriage with the King meant treading a careful religious tightrope. Bishop Gardiner watched her covertly as he harboured suspicions about her affiliations, but she was wise enough to provide no hostages to fortune. Privately she prayed for the souls of the three martyrs and hardly dared guess if theirs was so much worse a death than beheading. In fact by the standards of the time there were far more horrific deaths, chiefly hanging, then disembowelling whilst still alive. It needed a strong stomach to weather such foul tortures. Between the Papist sympathies of her late husband and the limited, reforming tendency of her present one she trod a narrow path of conformity to the prevailing ideology without nailing her colours to the mast. It was fortunate that tact and diplomacy formed a part of her personality and she harboured covert affiliations which could win more from circuitous reasoning than by frontal attack.

Once settled in the medieval fortress of Windsor Katharine turned her attentions once more to the King's three children who all lived away from the court.

'My lord it much troubles me that your children are separated from their dear father whom they must long to see. I too would be delighted to meet them and to learn how they are progressing with their studies. May I have your permission to write to them and to invite them to join us here at court?'

'Indeed sweetheart and you may treat them as the children you never had and keep them in holy and obedient ways'.

Elizabeth replied at once with delight, writing 'I await with much impatience the orders of the King my father for the accomplishment of the happiness for which I sigh, and I remain with much submission, Your Majesty's very dear Elizabeth'. Elizabeth had been much attached to Katherine Howard who had been an active and amusing companion and was deeply shocked by her execution, vowing never to marry herself. Her traumatic childhood had taught her the need for dissimulation and discretion and her sharp mind and love of learning had made her a precocious ten year old.

Katharine greeted her warmly and was pleased with her progress in the schoolroom, taking on herself the future course of her learning. Henry was so satisfied with her competence that he in turn asked her advice about Edward's tutors. With Mary, who was not so very much younger than her stepmother, Katherine too struck up a bond of friendship and side stepping the pitfalls of religious differences, they became firm friends. There was the tie of Katherine's age which was to cement their relationship and Katherine was pleased to show Mary the rosary of lignum given to her mother by Mary's mother. On holding this Mary wept openly and sobbed quietly.

'How I would have loved to have spent time with my mother who was so very unhappy. I would like to have been with her when she died, without my presence or that of any loved one. She had only servants to turn to in her hour of need. I could have prayed with her and brought her the comfort of Mother Church'. Katharine put her arm around Mary's shoulders and held her close.

They walked together in the garden and after some time Mary recovered her spirits a little as Katharine spoke.

'I am so very sorry Princess. Even if I had been then married to the King your father I doubt if I could have helped. It is very tragic but she is at peace now you know and we must hold that to our hearts. We women were born to obey dear Mary' she whispered. 'It must have been difficult being queen so far from home and her own people. She was always faithful to her beliefs and that was brave'.

Mary held back her tears as she turned and faced Katharine. 'I pray by the blood of Christ that my mother is at peace with the holy angels who surround the throne of God.' Katherine put her arms round her and decided to turn the conversation away from religious beliefs before a possible difference of opinion could arise.

'I am so pleased to see you at court Your Royal Highness and I think your royal father will be pleased with your proficiency in foreign tongues and your knowledge of history. He has been so longing to have you join him here. Try not to dwell too much on the past. It will only make you sad. If I may as a humble subject offer a word of caution?' Mary nodded but said nothing.

'Religion is a subject for faith and often not for discussion in public'. Mary looked hard at her but kept silent. She knew about the bond that had existed between her own mother and Katharine's mother and that her name linked them both and it caused a warm friendship between them. When they walked together in the garden Mary turned to Katharine with tears in her eyes again to Katharine's sorrow. She returned to her grievance. 'I did not see my own mother for years and I could not write to her often'. Katharine considered her answer and replied tactfully 'I think your dear father wished to keep you close to the court'. Mary looked at her quizzically and turned away dabbing her eyes.

'If I may as a humble subject, offer a word of advice would you be offended?'

'Speak on' murmured Mary.

'When you come to court it is wise not to initiate religious issues in my opinion. Some may disagree and take much offence'.

'I hope I shall be allowed to visit her tomb one day' whispered Mary. 'It is in Peterborough Cathedral'.

'Say no more Princess. We all may have different thoughts about that.'

'How I would love to visit my mother's country' she murmured and then changed the conversation.

'His Majesty your father and I would like you and the Princess to come and live with us at court. I would like to see how you are progressing with your reading dear Princess'. And so it was agreed to Katharine's deep pleasure that the family should be united. Sadly for Mary the pain she had suffered on being kept from her mother and her alienation from the growing spirit of religious reform were largely responsible for making her an embittered and narrow minded Queen and caused her to be known as 'Bloody Mary'.

With Edward too Katharine became friend and advisor and provided him with the stability that had been denied him. Mary and Edward could scarcely have been more divided in their religious views but the traumas of their childhoods had instilled in them the necessity of discretion and keeping their views to themselves. It was a testament to Katherine's marital diplomacy that peace reigned after the marriage, between husband and wife and between new mother and children.

Margaret Draper

Chapter 8 The French Adventure

Nevertheless, despite her empathy with the King, Queen Katherine might well have been deeply unsettled by the Act of Succession which was passed in 1544 by which any children of his marriage to Katharine or any other queens would succeed Edward to the throne. As they had been married for seven years with no heir could Henry be thinking of yet another marriage? Even more concerning to Katharine was the question of how he would proceed to take another consort whilst she lived. And yet Henry seemed content with his current wife and harmony reigned within his family group. The mention of 'other queens' gave Katharine sleepless nights when she considered how he had removed the queens before her. She drew comfort from his kindness towards her and was diligent never to cross him or for the moment, to delve too deeply into religious controversy.

He had for some time planned an invasion of France to teach that troublesome neighbour and old rival a salutary lesson and now that he apparently seemed settled in his marriage he spoke to Katharine when his plans were forming.

'I am minded to appoint you as Regent in my absence as a sign of my trust in you. You will have advisers but will have the final say in decisions.' Katharine was overwhelmed by this show of confidence in her and thanked her husband on her knees.

'It is the greatest honour Your Majesty and I will be sure to carry out the trust you show in me until your safe return'.
The Queen herself wrote a prayer for the King's safety which was read in churches as follows:-

O Almighty King and Lord of Hosts which by thy angels thereunto appointed dost minister both war and peace and which did give unto David both courage and strength being but a little one unarmed and inexpert in feats of war, to set upon and overthrow the great, huge Goliath; our course now being just and being enforced to enter into war and battle, we most humbly beseech thee O Lord God of Hosts, so to turn the hearts of our enemies to the desire of peace that no Christian blood be spilt or else grant O Lord, that with small effusion of blood and to the little hurt and damage of our men, we may to Thy glory and honour... with hearts and minds together in concord and unity...praise Thee which lives and reigns world without end Amen.'

Henry was rejuvenated at being at the head of his troops and made for France via Calais to settle scores with his old enemy. Katherine wrote a loving letter to him whilst he was away.
She said 'Although the distance and time and account of days neither is long nor many of your Majesty's absence, yet the want of your presence, so much desired and beloved by me, makes me that I cannot quietly pleasure in anything until I hear from your Majesty. The time seems to me very long, with a great desire to know how Your Highness hath done since your departing hence, whose prosperity and health I prefer and desire more than mine own...thus love makes me in all things set apart mine own convenience and pleasure and to embrace most joyfully his will and pleasure whom I love'. Katherine's

fulsome love letter belies her former reluctance to marry the King or is perhaps a testament to her increasing love for him that she could write thus 'God, the knower of secrets can judge these words to be written not only with ink, but most truly impressed in the heart'. Katherine had been left to head a council of five and she managed his affairs at home competently, sending him money, supplies and men. She also watched over his children with loving care and no doubt relished being in sole command. During the campaign there had been another outbreak of the plague and in addition to attending the affairs of state she had taken the children out of London into the country and then returned to London to continue with her regency duties.

Henry was meanwhile in his element reliving the days of his youth and led his army to besiege Boulogne and to attack the ramparts. Katherine gloried in his achievements but pleaded that 'no Christian blood should be spilt'.

On hearing of his success, she wrote to him that she was 'giving unto Almighty God most humble thanks' for his magnificent victory and she 'rejoiced at the joyful news' of his good health'. Henry wrote back addressing her as 'most dearly and entirely beloved wife'.

When his work in France was completed to his satisfaction Henry returned in triumph and Katherine hurried down to Dover to meet him. She had successfully deputised for him and his gratitude was palpable.

'My dear Lord' she almost sobbed when meeting him as he stepped onto English soil. 'How I have missed you and how I glory in your victory'.

He raised her up and kissed her warmly. 'Surely you did not doubt that we would be victorious? We put our faith in God and our righteous cause and we are rewarded by the Almighty'.

Katharine could scarcely stop smiling and praise for her regency filled her with joy. She had faced a demanding role and had succeeded and she could hardly recall that she had not wished to marry Henry. They made a triumphal progress at the head of the troops into London and were cheered by the townsfolk who were overjoyed at a victory on French soil. Since the time of Henry V it had been the ambition of successive kings to maintain their superiority over their troublesome neighbour. This was Henry's last martial excursion and he now could turn his thoughts to domestic matters and face a more peaceful home life with his admired queen and family.

However, there was a little matter with the Princess Elizabeth to be resolved. Some time before Henry had left for France there had been a falling out between himself and the Princess Elizabeth over an unknown matter and she had been sent away from the court. She was afraid to plead forgiveness from her father but approached Katharine to intercede for her.

'Your Majesty I have a favour to ask of you as I am so upset at the coolness of my dear father the King which hurts me dreadfully. I love him dearly and never meant to anger him'. Katharine had a warm spot for Elizabeth who was a hard working student in the classroom and was learning Latin and Italian
and proceeding well. Her first letter to her step-mother had been written in Italian. Katharine was keen to encourage Elizabeth to read the Bible and translate some of it herself into English. She knew some thought the Bible should not be read by the laity but that they should let the clergy read and interpret it for them. However she was a free thinker despite some disapproval and persevered with Elizabeth and Edward when she was allowed to, in encouraging them to read the Bible

for themselves. She loved to discuss religion with Henry although he sometimes was less studious in that respect than his offspring. He also had an innate suspicion and distrust of any woman taking on herself the interpretation of the Word of God. Katherine trod cautiously and was temperate in her opinions if possible.

Elizabeth had asked her step mother to write on her behalf when Henry was in France 'praying for his sweet benediction' and for God to send him victory 'so that your Highness and I may rejoice in his happy return'. Her prayer was granted and Henry had softened and allowed her to rejoin Katharine at her court at Greenwich. It would appear that campaigning had obviously agreed with Henry and gave him a new lease of life as his successful siege of Boulogne had worked well to the vast improvement of his temper. His letters addressing her as 'sweetheart' from 'your loving husband' were balm to the eyes of Katharine whose own calmness of spirit found solace in his and she hoped his softened temper would embrace Elizabeth too as it indeed appeared to in time.

When he had returned in triumph their pleasure in their reunion was evident for all to see and the King's pride in his wife's successful regency was a tribute to her capable management. She had proved efficient and competent in raising £40,000 to be sent to Henry in France and had expressed the most heartfelt joy at his success 'under God's bountiful care'.

'It was ordained no doubt of God' she said as she gloried in his success and Henry in his turn was proud of her regency and addressed her in his letter as 'most entirely and dearly beloved wife.' For once he could glory in the wife he had chosen who was not only loyal but also extremely capable and trustworthy in his absence.

Now with some leisure to attend to her own affairs at court Katharine was replacing those of her entourage who retired with ladies of a distinctly evangelical line of thought rather than their catholic predecessors. One observer commented that in her household
'Every day is like a Sunday, a thing hitherto unheard of especially in a palace.' This did not concern Henry at first when he had returned in triumph. The campaign had given him a new and zestful lease of life and he even went hunting for one more time and enjoyed the peace of family routine.

Despite the great success of the war regency Katharine was to find that marital waters were not always so calm in the following days. During Henry's absence she had supervised Elizabeth's classroom reading and it was perhaps she who introduced Elizabeth to a French poem called 'Miroir de l'ame pecheresse' (A mirror of the Sinful Soul) by Marguerite of Angouleme.' Despite being only eleven Elizabeth was a precocious student and decided to give the Queen a surprise.

'Dear Mother Queen I hope you will be pleased with something I have done especially for Your Majesty'. Perhaps it was a thank you present for the Queen's intercession with her father on her behalf when she had been removed from the court.

'I await it with interest Princess', replied the loving Katharine and was enchanted to receive the translation from her studious step daughter which included a dedication to herself.

'I do trust that the file of your most godly wit and excellent learning…..shall rub out, polish and mend…..the words or rather the order of my writing'. This dedication and the learned bent of her step-daughter were exactly to Katharine's own erudite taste and she lost no time in passing the book around chosen courtiers. It perhaps inspired the Queen to write her own book in 1654 which soon followed called 'Prayers stirring the Mind unto Heavenly Meditations' which ran through several editions and furthered Katharine's wish to stimulate reading of the Gospel.

When Henry had the leisure after his return he was faced with publications from his close family ladies which not only surprised and startled him in their Protestant leanings but also made him somewhat envious. The diehard old guard at court, traditionalists as they were in the palace, were disturbed by this radical stance and looked around for means of bringing them back into line. Chief amongst these was Wriothesley the Chancellor. It was perhaps hints of his to the King which made him somewhat jealous and suspicious of his wife's success as the book ran into several editions. However for the moment he bided his time.

Chapter 9 Stepmother to Future King and Queens

Katharine's other admirer returned about that time after completing his present term of office in The Netherlands. He lost no time in meeting up with Katherine and recounting his occupations abroad. Although she still harboured affectionate feelings for her former suitor, she did not forget the fate of Anne Boleyn and kept a certain aloofness whilst taking care only to meet with Thomas in public places.

'Well Sir Thomas how did you enjoy the beer and the cheeses in the Netherlands? Were you received well and with loyal sentiments towards His Majesty?' Thomas smiled and turned to his pressing query.

'How does His Majesty this many a day?' he enquired. He refrained from asking the question which nagged his mind about life with the King from Katherine's point of view. Instead he queried 'Will he be well enough to receive me soon do you think? Will you smooth the path of my return to court and mention my name to His Majesty as begging an audience?'

'Indeed His Majesty is in fair health and good spirits and I will tell him about your return and that you beg to report to him' she replied and then seeing the Lord Chancellor eyeing them from across the hall, she swept him a curtsy and added in a voice that could easily be heard 'Lose no time in requesting an audience with the King in a day or two when I have informed him of your return' and she quickly left the room.

Henry viewed Seymour with mixed feelings and neatly forestalled any renewal of his infatuation with Katherine by appointing him Lord High Admiral which conveniently removed him from the scene of action. Perhaps Henry had a sense of humour alongside his shrewdness as Seymour was not known for his love of the sea. He no doubt had a quiet chuckle to himself as Seymour expressed his gratitude for the unsought honour.

Katharine at that time won plaudits from the Spanish Emperor via his ambassador Capuys. 'I am ordered to thank you on behalf of the Emperor for the kind care and help that you have given to the Princess Mary.'

'Ambassador Capuys, it is the least I can do for her late mother's sake after whom I am named. I almost fancifully think of the Princess Mary as my kin for whom I bear responsibility, though indeed I know I cannot claim that honour. Nevertheless whatever I can do for her it is my duty and my pleasure for His Majesty's sake'. Despite her Protestant leanings Katherine had the maturity to encourage amity between England and Spain and as she hoped to Capuys 'God would avert the slightest dissensions as friendship is so vital to both countries'. Capuys himself was not well and was due to retire to his native Spain and Henry who was also indisposed, deputed Katharine to thank him and bid him farewell. This she did most graciously saying 'The King thanks you and has trusted you and he hopes that your health will be better in warmer climes'. Capuys was charmed by Katharine, who although she did not share his religion did not let that stand in the way of her genuine respect and thanks.

Elizabeth too loved and respected her step mother and in presenting her with her translation of 'Le Miroir de l'Ame Pecheresse' wrote the following dedication - 'To the Most Noble and Virtuous Queen Katharine her humble daughter wishes perpetual happiness and everlasting joy'. Elizabeth's studious nature and mastery of languages were to stand her in good stead in the life that fate would hand out to her and she always took pride in her ability to speak other tongues.

The young Prince Edward too was influenced by Katharine's care for his studies. He was a delicate and precocious child, serious and dignified and carefully guarded from illness and with his wellbeing Katharine was always concerned.

As well as encouraging her step children's studies and translations Katherine at this time produced a small book called 'Prayers and Meditations' and with it came the blessing of the King. It was so well received that Katherine garnered honours from both universities of Oxford and Cambridge, becoming their Patroness. The scholar, Roger Ascham, wrote to this royal blue stocking 'We rejoice vehemently in your happiness, most happy Princess, because you are learning more amidst the occupations of your dignity than many of us do in all our leisure and quiet.' Her household became a centre of learning and there was keen competition to gain a place in it and to profit thereby. The calm that Katharine worked for was a blessing superficially but in Henry's life still waters never excluded hidden depths of storm and fear and she and others at court, had to keep a keen eye open for ferocious upsets caused by jealous observers not averse to fomenting trouble.

Nor did she neglect the children of the tenants and workers on the royal estates. She called the Archbishop of Canterbury, Matthew Parker, in to discuss her plans.

'I know Master Parker that you served the late Queen Anne Boleyn when she needed learned advice'. Matthew bowed in acknowledgement.

'What I have in mind and His Majesty has approved this, is to draw up a pattern of learning for the workers on the estate. It must be practical needless to say, but must also include some religious instruction as befits those who labour for His Majesty. I dare say that this is a new concept for a learned scholar like yourself but I hope you will be able to give me advice and to provide some supervision.' Her genuine love of learning was strange in a woman in those days and Katherine was fortunate in being able to initiate this unusual scheme at her own expense. There were some unkind onlookers who called her the royal bluestocking, but Katherine was generally unaware of them.

Although the King's health had been so robust when campaigning in France, that had been his swansong and it took a turn for the worse in 1545 when he was laid low with his painful leg which even the new Spanish ambassador thought might be his undoing.

The Queen spent time sitting with him and stimulating his mind by theological discussions which he had always encouraged but there were others listening in who viewed her opinions with distrust on account of her growing leaning towards Protestantism. Katharine was somewhat taxed as to the subjects of discussion that would arouse the interest of the King. He was not greatly interested in art and literature and in religion predominantly he was concerned with maintaining his authority in its dogma. The Bible and religion seemed a safe subject but it held hidden pitfalls.

'Your Majesty would help me if you are so inclined with a question that sometimes troubles me'.

'What is that Katharine?' he enquired with interest.

'Can we ask for God's forgiveness and succour by praying to Him directly or must we have a priest as intercessor?'

'Why do you ask Katharine? Have you something that weighs heavy on your spirit?'

'We all have sinned Your Majesty and I am not least a sinner.'

'It is not only priests that can offer prayers' pronounced the King.

'As a child I was taught always to seek intercession' said Katharine.

'Priests are not the only way to God, though they would like to be' replied the King somewhat testily.

At that moment a spasm seized him and he clutched his leg in pain.

'Come Katherine and help me to my apartments where you can bathe my leg. What pain it gives me day and night'. Leaning on Katharine's shoulder and with attendants solicitous to help he hobbled off to leave the religious exchange for another time. The task of bathing the King's suppurating and noisome leg was not a task sought by anyone, but whoever took on the role had to be careful not to show any disgust or loathing. Katherine proved to be a kind and understanding nurse.

However, she was not without enemies of the Catholic persuasion who thought that she had sympathies with Protestant heretics. Staunch Catholics like Gardiner and Wriosthesley feared her undue influence over the King and discussed the matter between themselves in the privacy of the gardens.

'Queen Katharine takes too much on herself' said Gardiner. 'It seems that she is drunk with power after her regency during the French campaign. Then she took on herself to rule the country. Now she thinks she is God's chosen messenger'. Wriosthesley was also beginning to temper his former admiration of the Queen and it seemed that in the court of King Henry to express any religious opinion was to walk a tightrope of danger. Ever since Henry had turned to the newly translated Bible to give him the authority to divorce Katherine of Aragon, he had been a keen student of its word in any matter where authority was in question and to Henry it was his authority and interpretation which held sway. Those in the hierarchy of the English church under Henry might well feel that their position was being undermined but they fostered a diplomatic taciturnity.

Unbeknown to Katharine the Chancellor had information which he hoped might unseat this over enquiring Queen and he was not averse to using it. Approaching Katharine as she left the King he asked to have a word with her. Graciously the Queen agreed and withdrew to a quiet window seat beckoning him to be seated.

'Your Majesty I know that you love above all things to hold discussions on religion'. Katherine sensed danger from her old adversary and replied carefully. 'Do we not all Lord Chancellor? His Majesty is pleased above all things to encourage his court to adhere to the truth'. Wriosthesley tried again.

'Does Your Majesty recall the name Anne Askew?'

'Indeed no my Lord. How should I be supposed to know that name?'

'We have had occasion to put this woman under arrest and she admits she has sent you heretical books about the Protestant

religion'. Katharine rose with spots of colour burning her cheeks. 'My lord I take this approach of yours as very uncivil and I shall raise this matter with His Majesty'. Wriosthesley arose too bowing and saying 'His Majesty is already aware of this heretic woman and is deeply concerned about her'.
'This has nothing to do with me my Lord and I bid you good day', said the Queen gathering her dress and leaving the Lord Chancellor with a frosty bow.

Poor Anne Askew was taken to the Tower where she was tortured on the rack with the Lord Chancellor turning the wheel himself until she was left broken boned and unable to stand. Her fate was sealed by her answers and she was carried to her execution because she was unable to walk to her death; which death must have been a blessed relief.

The contagion of suspicion of Katherine's over zealous championing of the Protestant cause reached Henry and he too weighed her views and found them wanting.
'I do not need my wife or any woman to tell me what I should believe' he said testily to her when they had been discussing religious matters.
'Indeed not Your Majesty' replied Katharine, adding tactfully 'You are the arbiter of opinion to me and all the court.' Henry's ulcerated leg did not improve his temper but Katharine's modesty won him round usually and he left calling her 'Sweetheart'. Warning bells rang in Katharine's ears, as she knew how quickly Henry's love could turn to hate. Bishop Gardiner added fuel to the flames saying that he could 'make great discoveries if he were not deterred by the Queen's powerful faction' and warned Henry of cherishing 'a serpent within his own bosom'.

In fact the serpent in the King's bosom was Gardiner himself who lost no opportunity of adding fuel to the flames of Henry's disagreements with Katharine's views. He prompted Henry's dislike of being contradicted. When Henry grumbled 'A good hearing it is when women become such clerks and much to my comfort in my old age to be taught by my wife' Gardiner happily agreed.

Katharine stood in danger and she knew it. The King no longer made his daily visits to her apartments and it remained for her to visit him and face his black moods and general irritability. For the first time Katharine felt seriously and dangerously threatened and after further consultations with Gardiner Henry decided to arrest three of Katharine's ladies and planned to put the Queen on trial.

He issued and signed a warrant for Katharine's arrest which was carelessly dropped on the floor and was found by a servant of Katharine's and brought to her. 'Your majesty' he said handing the incriminating document to her. 'I found this in the great chamber and seeing that it concerned Your Majesty I have brought it straightaway to your eyes'. Katharine trembled with shock as she read the accusations from Bishop Gardiner. She thought for a moment that she was going to faint. However she did not lose her nerve and told her servant, having absorbed its accusations, to return it to the same place. The shock to Katharine was nevertheless overwhelming as she saw herself following Anne Boleyn and Katharine Howard to the block. She sat down heavily with her head in her hands. 'What had brought her to this pass?' she asked herself. She did not have to look far for the answer. She had not committed adultery like Anne Boleyn nor had lovers before her marriage like Katharine Howard; she had not challenged Henry on religious matters and divorce like her namesake Katharine of

Aragon – or had she? Was it not her religious discussions with Henry which leant towards the type of Protestantism that he abhorred that had brought this tension to their marriage? No doubt Gardiner the Bishop of Winchester was glad to stoke the fires of dispute and question her authority. Was she destined to tread the soft grass of Tower Green to the hard blade on the block? She felt her neck gingerly and shuddered.

Returning to her private apartments she sank into a chair and began sobbing uncontrollably. Her sobs turned to screams until the King himself hearing her, sent his doctor to minister to her. The Queen was inconsolable and eventually Henry made his way to her room where her genuine grief moved him to forgiveness. Katharine, recalling the fate of Anne Askew vowed to meddle no more in religious matters nor would she seek to dispute on religion with the King again. She sought the King out in his bedchamber that evening and was careful to say nothing contentious, adding that God had appointed Henry as supreme head of the church and that she would always learn from him. 'I am a woman' she added 'with all the imperfections natural to my sex' and that Henry was her 'lord and master'.

'Sweetheart' said Henry 'then we are perfect friends' and he kissed her in front of all those present. Katharine knelt at his feet and kissed his hands murmuring 'my lord and master'.

The following day when Henry and Katharine were taking the air Gardiner and the Lord Chancellor appeared with guards to arrest Katharine but the reconciled King turned on him calling him 'an arrant fool' and dismissed him. Henry took Katherine in his arms and said 'On my word, sweetheart, he hath been to thee an arrant knave'.

Katherine could have sobbed with relief and tried to put away the thought of the close brush she had had with an appalling end.

Chapter 10 Death of the King

Katherine's time with Henry was coming to a close as his health took a turn for the worse. He spent Christmas apart from her at Whitehall whereas she remained at Greenwich. They had always spent the festive season together previously but perhaps the recent rift between them had left its mark. Although the Queen was planning to move to Whitehall and her rooms were being prepared, she did not see Henry again until just before his death in her arms on 28 January 1547. Still of sound mind he enjoined the Council 'to treat her as if I were living still' and if she should remarry she was to receive £7000 and all her jewels. This was a generous gesture as he probably guessed that her choice would fall on Thomas Seymour, no friend of his. Before his death he had made his will and in it Katharine was to take no regency or governing role as Queen Mother. The power which he had invested in her during his French campaign had perhaps eroded with some religious differences since then. But maybe the main reason was that if Katherine were in a position of power then Seymour would not be far behind. He left his kingdom and power to Prince Edward followed by the two princesses and then to any of his children that 'our entirely beloved Queen Katharine' might have after his death. Of his Queen he praised 'the great love, obedience, chastity of life and wisdom' she had shown, leaving her whatever she desired of his valuable wardrobe. She was also to receive £1000 in cash as her dower from Parliament.

   Henry had selected those who would serve on the regency Council which was notable for its reformist views. With his dying breath he refused to allow Thomas Seymour to serve, thus finally putting him in his place as perhaps his lasting jealousy dictated. He requested the reformist Cramner to pray for him by his deathbed. Although he had been an English Catholic King to the end it was as if he foresaw the scales swinging towards Protestantism after his death.   Henry's departure was, as his life, a semi public affair and there was no such thing as an intimate leave taking between husband and wife without an audience.

   Despite his often cruel punishments he was in truth only the mirror of his age which considered tolerance as a weakness. Neither the young King Edward nor his sisters the Princesses Mary and Elizabeth attended their father's funeral. Katherine was not permitted as a woman to attend Henry's burial though she prayed by his body before it was prepared for its final journey. She wondered what would become of her, despite the King's generous provision for her as a widow, alone and helpless as she would be. She asked her brother William to visit her after the funeral to describe the day to her. Before he came to her she had overheard a snatch of conversation about the funeral day which somewhat alarmed her and made her anxious to speak to her brother as soon as possible. He visited her at Hampton Court two days later and was shocked by her wan appearance. 'You must not make yourself ill' he said as he gently kissed her. 'The King would not have wished it you know'.

'What happened William?' she said. 'Did all go smoothly for my dear Lord?'
'The service was dignified and there were many laudatory expressions indeed.'
'But something unusual and bad occurred. I heard a snatch of conversation'.
'You must not fret my sister' replied Lord Essex as he was now called. 'But I cannot help it. Oh do, do tell me William. He was my own husband'.
'Take a seat sister' said William. 'I will tell you all. Try not to be too upset. Overnight His Majesty's body rested at Syon Abbey, for with the long procession it was a slow progress to arrive there. During the night the lead coffin burst open and.'.....
Katherine gasped at this but signalled him to continue. 'It had heavy contents as you would imagine and the lead could not contain it. His Majesty's blood seeped through to the floor of the chapel and a dog was found licking it up'. Katharine gasped and swayed forward but William held her in his arms. 'It was said that this fulfilled a prophecy that if the King cast off Katharine of Aragon and married Anne Boleyn, the dogs would lick up his blood'.
'And then what happened?' 'King Henry was buried at Windsor and..'

'With ,with his wife Jane Seymour' sobbed Katharine and burst into floods of tears.

'This was his will dear sister, you must not sorrow so' said William and tried his best to comfort the inconsolable widow, but despite his great effort at kindness he was unable to stop Katharine's floods of tears and in the end he sent for her ladies to escort her to her chamber.

Chapter 11 Leave the Court

Katherine could not stay in her apartments feeling so unsettled. She wandered round the grounds like a lost soul thinking about the past and wondering what the future would bring. Edward being now King would have his own ideas and was thought to be devoutly Protestant and not likely to favour Catholics. Would he persecute them as Lutheran Protestants had been during Henry's reign? She thought with a shudder of the three Protestants who were burnt to death at Windsor Castle to celebrate her marriage. She tried not to think of the Protestant who was chained up by his arms above a bonfire which slowly and agonisingly roasted him to death. Yet Henry had not been altogether intolerant and had mellowed somewhat during his reign. She knew that Princess Mary was an unflinchingly devout Catholic though she had not flaunted her beliefs. Would Edward tolerate this? There was no easy solution and the turmoil in her mind with recent widowhood was aggravated by the tumultuous thoughts of the future and gave her no peace. 'Your Majesty' said her lady 'we have been looking for you in the gardens and throughout the state rooms. Do come with me and be comforted by your ladies who feel so much for your sorrow'. Katharine was led away gently and back to her own apartments where she sat and gazed dully through the window.

'We are all sad for you Your Majesty' said her most intimate lady. 'What can we do to make your spirits heal? Would you like us to pray with you or to play some soft music?' Katharine turned to look at her and said blankly 'He expressly omitted me from the Council as if he did not trust me'. The ladies glanced at each other anxiously and one of them spoke up quietly.
'Your Majesty a lady is never allowed to join the Council. It is not done. Do not be saddened because of that for indeed His Majesty loved you and left you well apportioned'.
'When he went to France to do battle against his old enemy, he left me in sole charge and responsible for dispensing funds and sending him supplies. Now I am nothing – just the last of his wives and of no account. He left me his garments with all their jewels for which I am grateful. The King left me alone and at the mercy of others who may be jealous'.

She sobbed quietly and thought about Anne, wife of the Protector and her enemy without a doubt despite being her sister-in-law. She would no doubt be further ennobled with her husband and become even more unbearable. The sooner she left the court the better it would be for her. She tried to pull herself together and smiled wanly at her ladies. Life would go on but the shock had to be borne. When she was alone again she thought back to the reason for the conditions of Henry's will. The truth struck her with the force of a hammer blow. Henry had always been rather antagonistic towards Thomas Seymour with his apparent affection for his wife. He would imagine as he approached death that Seymour would step forward and claim his hitherto forbidden prize. If Katherine capitulated whatever she owned would be his. That would be anathema to Henry and he therefore restricted Katherine's share of his wealth. The more she thought about it the more logical it seemed. The last thing Henry would have desired was

Thomas Seymour claiming to rule the country. He trusted rather his brother who was not the ladies' man that Thomas undoubtedly was. Henry was motivated by jealousy thought Katharine and strangely when she faced this fact she felt considerably heartened. After all he was paying her a compliment of sorts and although not his foremost inheritor she would never lack for means. The ladies came back silently to see how their mistress was faring. She seemed somewhat more settled.

They looked at each other anxiously and after a few minutes one of them spoke up. 'Your Majesty forgive me please but take heart from this thought. You are the only Queen and royal wife to survive His Majesty. There were others who would have thought themselves to be fortunate indeed to have survived and in the departing King's good graces'.

There was a silence from Katherine and the ladies waited for a reprimand as having exceeded their duties. Instead the Queen looked at them and tried to force a smile. 'I know you mean to comfort me and I welcome your kindness, but do not repeat what you have just said to anyone. It might be misconstrued and may lead to no good consequences as I am sure you understand. Time is a great healer and my comfort is in the Lord of Hosts. My dear departed Lord meant well and gave consideration to his wishes. I am content. Now I give you leave to leave me for I wish to pray for guidance'. The ladies curtseyed without speaking and withdrew.

Katherine was free to re-marry if she would and could afford to live where she liked and do as she wished. However the Regency Council took care that she should not have access to the young King Edward V1 much to her sorrow. They were determined that the new, young King should be subject to their influence alone. Edward also was upset that he could not have the company of the Queen Dowager who had been a kindly surrogate mother to him. When talking to the Lord Protector he brought his concerns to the fore.

'My lord I wish to speak to my Mother Queen and to share her grief with her'.

'Your Majesty, we must protect you from all outside influences until you reach your majority. Then of course, you will be the dictator of what it is wise to do'.

Both Katharine and the young King considered these restrictions as not what the late King would have decreed, but power had shifted now to the Regency Council and they must follow its precepts. Edward however was allowed to write to Katharine and express his sadness. 'Farewell venerated Queen' he wrote in Latin in a letter that she treasured all her life. It was a foretaste of Edward's short and lonely life that he was guarded and separated from his loving step-mother.

Not only did the Council jealously guard the King but they also bestowed honours on themselves on the very day of King Henry's funeral. Katherine's brother William was to be the Lord Essex still and to receive the Garter. Katharine's old admirer Thomas Seymour became Baron Sudeley of Sudeley Castle in Gloucestershire and Lord High Admiral still as well as receiving the Order of the Garter. Thomas's brother the Earl of Hertford now became 1st Duke of Somerset and of course Lord Protector. Seymour was far from pleased that, as the King's uncle, he was barred from sitting on the ruling Council. The Council, however, were revelling in their new found and unrestricted authority. They did not want the King's Uncle Thomas sitting on the Council with all the authority he might claim in kinship with the King. Also the Lord Protector's wife Anne disliked Thomas intensely and doubtless made her feelings known to her husband. She revelled in the position her husband now had and the authority she could claim as his wife.

Katharine had it in her own hands as to where she would like to live and thought back to the contented days she had spent in Chelsea with her second husband Lord Latimer and also to the times there with the King in the house he had built for Jane Seymour. Those had been contented and carefree times on the whole and she thought to relive happier days by settling there which would be a comfort to her.

However before she had actually moved she was visited by the new Baron Sudeley, Thomas Seymour in his previous incarnation. Sudeley felt he had been denied power and poured his heart out to his old admirer.

'What a pleasure it is to meet up again Your Majesty' he said bowing low and kissing her hand with some fervour. 'I give my commiserations to Your Majesty on the sad demise of your husband the King.'

'Indeed Thomas you are very kind and I congratulate you on your new honours which are long overdue'.

Thomas looked down unhappily, 'It is my rightful place to be on the Council. The King was not thinking when he left me off. I know whom to blame for this omission, the new Duchess of Somerset, Anne'.

'Hush my dear Lord, you must not say that to anyone. It will do you no good and may in fact bring you harm.'

'Let us retire to that window seat where we can catch up on our lives again'. He led Katharine to the arbour of some privacy and gazed into her eyes with passion.

'Well Thomas now you have been made Lord High Admiral for life amongst other honours much deserved, will you be leaving once again to sail the seas?'

'Certainly not Katherine if I may call you that. I intend to stay in this country for as long as possible. I have no love for the sea and in fact feel quite ill when crossing the channel. I always felt it was a cruel joke to make me Lord High Admiral. It was an appointment I had to accept reluctantly but did not relish. Someone who shall remain unnamed has an unpleasant sense of humour'. He looked at her for some moments saying nothing until he whispered 'how I missed you'.

'You know that I was a faithful and loving wife to His Majesty and I did my duty when called'.

'Now you can choose for yourself' said Thomas and smiled winningly at Katharine who half turned to look out of the window.

'I am moving as soon as I may to Old Chelsea' said Katherine. 'It is a house I know and love and the late King has left it for me to use or to sell. I have decided to keep it as it has happy memories for me in my widowhood.'

'You will let me come and see you Katharine I trust?' said Thomas and again lifted her hand and kissed it.

'You will be my honoured guest. I hope also that the Princess Elizabeth will make her home with me. I intend to discuss the matter with her again as she is considering what she should do for the best. I trust I am allowed to speak to her and she is not kept away from me as is Prince or rather King Edward my dear stepson.'

'Will you first of all be my honoured guest at Sudeley Castle and give me advice on how I should improve and furnish it?'

'I will indeed do that but I intend to appear without delay in court wearing the jewels that my King and husband has left me and to bid farewell to those lords who have given me support in my sad time.'

Katherine felt that she should appear in state to the lords and their ladies rather than to disappear without a departing audience. She sent a request to Lord Somerset to send for her jewels from the Tower so that she could make a grand final entry in state. She awaited the jewels in her chamber and sent a message to his wife to do her the honour of bearing her train.

The Duchess of Somerset, relishing her new title, was far from pleased by this request and summoned her husband to attend her. Her husband was not reassured by the peremptory message but knowing his wife's unpredictable temper he hurried to meet her.

'My Lord I am much insulted. Am I to bear this indignity?'

'What indignity is that my love?' queried her husband anticipating a storm.

'The Dowager Queen orders me to bear her train when she appears in court. I am the first lady of the land now that you are the Lord Protector.'

'Could you not humour her this once Anne?' he pleaded. 'You know this is to be her last appearance at court and she intends to retire to the quietness of Chelsea'.

'I will not attend the court then' almost shouted his wife. The Duke capitulated in the interests of a quiet life.

'I will send a message to Her Majesty to tell her that you regret that you cannot oblige her as you are the wife of the Lord Protector and will have a train yourself'. Anne gave a faint smile of satisfaction and added 'I shall require the jewels from the Tower to wear myself as you are now the ruler of the kingdom in the King's minority'. Her husband sighed heavily and nodded his agreement. Then congratulated himself on his diplomacy and made a rapid exit.

Anne then sent a note to Katherine saying that as the wife of the Lord Protector she was now chief lady in the land and the jewels were at her own disposal until the King took a wife.

Katherine was furious at the indignities heaped upon her in her time of sorrow but she determined to appear as she had arranged and to ignore The Duchess as much as possible. She decided that she would be well quit of the Court and the arrogant Protector and his wife though she would not give up the battle for the jewels so easily.

She did not tarry long after saying her farewells and retired to her apartments in well disguised fury. She called Thomas Seymour to her to relate the humiliation she had suffered.

'Indeed I will travel with you to Sudeley and when I return it shall not be to Whitehall but to Old Chelsea. I shall be glad to get away from the court altogether. I shall be ready to accompany you after I have arranged for my wardrobe and valuables to be moved to Old Chelsea. I am glad to say that my request to the Council to let the Princess Elizabeth come to live with me has been granted'.

'And the Princess Mary?' queried Thomas.

'I do not think that the Princess would want to live with me much as I like and respect her. Her religion is far removed from my own and she would not find it to her taste. We have been close and I love her very much but our religious divide has become wider and deeper. Also she is now heiress to the throne and I am sure the Council will like to watch carefully over her'.

Thomas was disappointed about the Princess Mary but delighted with Katharine's willingness to visit his new castle and at once began to make plans for the journey to Gloucestershire.

When by herself after Thomas's departure she thought over his annoyance in not being allowed to be a Council member and requested her brother William's company to make further enquiries.

William was now a great man, thanks largely to the late King and also his sister's position as Queen Dowager but he was not inclined to further the cause of Seymour, to Katharine's disappointment.

'Baron Sudeley has been granted an elevation and a grand property and should be more than delighted to have such honours. In truth the late King, I am told, was in no wise minded to grant him further advancement and it would be against his wishes to alter his last will'.

'You are my brother, William, and would always give me good advice I trust. Were you privy to the late King's thoughts on the subject?'

'Indeed not Katharine and I can say no more except that it is thought that his influence over King Edward might not be encouraged. He is perhaps not without ambition'.

Katharine had to be content with that but she felt that Thomas was not considered the man to help rule and with that information she had to make her own judgement. However she knew that she found him amusing and good company and she could relax with him without having to guard her tongue and her feelings. She knew she was drifting inexorably towards marriage with him. She could not help dwelling on the fact that both she and Thomas were not wanted at court and may as well accept that fact. She mused on the unpleasant possibility that Thomas was interested in the future of the heiress to the throne and also her sister Elizabeth and tried not to think that he might be using her, Katharine, as a stepping stone to greater intimacy with either one of them. He had been denied power by the late King but may have ambitions to snatch at power through Mary or Elizabeth. Surely he could not be so devious? Did he not love her?

  She spent the following week supervising the removal of her belongings to Chelsea and also choosing which of the late King's clothes she would take with her according to his last wishes. When she handled them she felt the tears welling up again and was thankful for his generosity to her in the gifts he had left for her. As is the case with the death of a loved one, she found the good memories thankfully eclipsed the unhappy ones which she was glad to relegate to the back of her mind. She realised that her discussions with him on religion had perhaps gone too far and thankfully appreciated his tolerance towards her forward thinking. On the whole he had been good and kind to her despite the nagging pain in his leg which often accounted for his irritability. She determined to put the past behind her and to entertain thoughts of the future which she was still young enough to relish.

Chapter 12 Sudeley Castle

She and Thomas travelled out to Sudeley after two weeks had passed and she felt the relief of being able to be herself and to relax. Thomas was an entertaining companion and nothing he would do or say could threaten her peace of mind on the journey.

The castle of Sudeley was built in a most beautiful setting with the rolling, wooded hills around it and the soft countryside of fertile fields and meadows before it. Even in its present rather neglected state there was a feeling of tranquillity which was entirely beguiling. They were told that in the days of Roman occupation this had been the site of a great camp and villa and that there were remains of the villa in the woods above the castle. There was a high tower which they climbed up, stopping half way to recover their breath before reaching the top. The view round about was splendidly fertile and a pleasanter domain could hardly be envisaged. The castle needed some renovation which Thomas intended to put in hand without delay.

'This will in time be a fitting home for you Thomas and I shall look forward to visiting it when I feel the need to rest after life in busy London. Meanwhile you are welcome to visit me at

Chelsea often and to tell me how your improvements here are progressing'.

'I shall be happy to take you at your word Katherine and with great pleasure. There is much to be done here as it has seen many owners; one by the name of King Richard 111. The little chapel has been sadly neglected and the gardens are in much need of a lady's help in the planning'.

Before they left and as the weather was so pleasantly warm without being oppressive they decided to walk through the meadows up to the woods to look for the Roman remains if they were visible. A caretaker from the castle accompanied them to show them the way. The route was not difficult and with the birds singing around them and a pleasant breeze to cool them they came across the foundations of the villa without difficulty. To Katharine it was a magical and unforgettable little expedition and with the charms of Sudeley surrounding her, she felt the draw of London less powerful than previously. She hoped that the ghost of King Richard 111 did not remain to spoil the atmosphere of enchantment.

Katharine foresaw many idyllic times here, free of responsibility and cares and was only too happy to offer her advice if it might be sought.

'I believe' she said 'that King Henry brought his unfortunate Queen Anne Boleyn here in happier times. It would perhaps be wise not to take the Princess Elizabeth to your castle. The memory of her dead mother having been there in pleasanter times might distress her'.

'I doubt that she would know that her mother had visited here when she was only a baby. We will make our own happy memories here when you bless me with your company'. They did not stay at the castle long for indeed it was somewhat in need of improvement to make it welcoming as a home. After an uncomfortable night in a local hostelry they made their way back to London with its crowded streets, echoing street cries and pervasive smells.

Despite his recently renewed overtures to Katharine, Thomas also set his sights on a higher target. His lack of power rankled with him and he was deeply jealous of his brother being on the Council when he was excluded. He also suspected William Somerset's wife Anne was in part responsible with her jealous and overbearing influence. He chewed the matter over in his solitude and determined to acquire power by other means. The young King had two sisters and through them he might achieve his aims despite his promises to Katharine. Mary was a determined Catholic which made her less than desirable to Thomas but Elizabeth was a striking golden headed teenager with much of her beautiful mother's attractiveness and intelligence. Her religion, he believed was less over-riding and more inclined to the new Protestantism than Catholicism. He made up his mind to approach her as a delightful stepping stone to power. To be uncle to the king was good but not good enough. How might his influence increase if he were to be married to the Princess?

He allowed himself to dream and thought that with the Princess Elizabeth as his wife the world would be his oyster. How much more attractive she would be than William's acerbic and bitter spouse and how he would show off his beautiful wife and make jealous his opponents. He wrote enigmatically to her asking 'if I am to be the happiest or most miserable of men'. His thinly veiled proposal, however it may have flattered the young Elizabeth, was doomed to failure. Elizabeth was nobody's fool and she knew that she would have to obtain the permission of the Council to wed. She was acutely conscious of Thomas's charm and good looks but did not ignore his shallowness and ambition. It was very likely that from what she had experienced in her young life, she had a jaundiced view of matrimony. Why should marriage be any kinder to her than to her late mother? Would she not be safer trusting herself all her life than putting her faith in power hungry men of any cloth?

'My lord Seymour, if I may so address you, you must know that I am too young to marry and must wait for at least two years'. To drive the point home she wrote him courteously but decidedly. Her faith in men was doubtless jaded and born of experience albeit she was young. She added 'neither my age nor my inclination allows me to think of marriage'. Thomas was set back by the refusal but he had other lines of approach which he planned for the time when Katharine should be established in Old Chelsea. This time he kept his plans hidden away from everyone.

Elizabeth enjoyed, as her mother had, a flirtation but the wisdom which was to carry her through the vicissitudes of ruling was already a part of her personality. Although she had been a baby when her mother was beheaded she had gleaned enough information of her demise to realise that a charming manner must be backed by a hard headed determination to survive. Eventual marriage to a handsome and ambitious man could well lead her into dangerous waters and the only person she could truly trust was herself.

She added, to make herself crystal clear 'Permit me my Lord Admiral, to tell you frankly that, though I decline the happiness of becoming your wife, I shall never cease to interest myself in all that can crown your merit with glory, and shall ever feel the greatest pleasure in being your servant and good friend.'

Notwithstanding her clear headed assessment of Thomas, she nevertheless found the attention of an older man intriguing and was not averse to indulging in some light hearted flirtation.
He had a disconcerting propensity to appear silently behind her when she was reading and to blow on her neck. When she turned round startled he would catch her by the elbows and kiss her despite her squealing protests.
'My lord Seymour you gave me such a fright'.
'Hush my lady, do you want everyone to come running?'
'No indeed my lord. The Queen would not be best pleased'.
'I promise I will not do that again – only if you call me 'Thomas."
Elizabeth giggled and nodded her head in agreement. However he did not repeat that startling trick but tried something else. He would sidle up behind her and gently pull one of her golden tresses making her grab her hair and the hand holding it as well.
'My lord, I mean Thomas, I beg you not to do that again'. He would laugh quietly and promise no such thing.

His behaviour did not go unnoticed by Katharine's ladies and they consulted together as to what action to take.
'The Queen will hardly believe us if we tell her and she will be very angry' said one.
'She is bound to see him or hear them before too long. Let us not get involved unless she asks us directly'.
Probably at that time Elizabeth did not know about the possible marriage of Sudeley to her step-mother but even when that decision came to pass it did not prevent his provocative dalliance with her.

Elizabeth eventually called a halt to this dalliance and let Thomas know that it was by her rules that he would have to play if he wanted to enjoy her company. If only her mother had had her daughter's circumspection!

 He speculated on Mary's reaction if he should attempt flirtatious dalliance with her. Think on it as he might he could not envisage the serious and dour Mary reacting with anything other than scorn. That way danger lay!

Chapter 13 The Jealous Duchess

However he still had Katharine to pursue and wherever she might be it was probable that Elizabeth would not be far away. He decided that the next best outcome would be to wed Katharine and he determined to pursue this object which he did not imagine would be difficult.

Katharine was at this time still in mourning for the King and however much she might like to renew the attentions of an old flame, she had to be sure that the Council did not get wind of her pleasures. Nevertheless she decided that Thomas should be her next husband.

She could not resist confiding in an old friend Lady Paget, who counselled caution when she wrote to her.   'All I wish you Madam is that he should become your husband.' To which Katharine replied that she wished 'it had been her fate to have him for a husband'. Fortunately for Katherine these letters were kept strictly private. To Thomas she was more restrained.

 'My dear lord, your offer has given me much food for thought but now it is spring and I must finish furnishing Old Chelsea to my taste. As I am still in mourning it would be unthinkable to marry yet a while'. Despite this Katharine was enthralled to have this last chance of true love, though her husband had only been buried six weeks ago. She also felt that the Council would be against her marrying Sudeley.

For his part Thomas could not wait to make Katharine's position and prestige his own too and urged marriage in secret. The Council would have had other difficulties to raise at this hasty marriage. As the King had only been dead for such a short time, it was not impossible that Katharine might be pregnant with another heir to the throne after Edward.

Sudeley felt himself blocked at every turn and in desperation decided to ask the young King for his permission. The young King had a great deal of affection for his handsome and amusing uncle but Sudeley considered that this avenue would be blocked to him as access to the young King was being closely monitored. He decided on a risky and daring plan to approach the King clandestinely and turn his back on the stuffy Council. What did those pedantic men know of true love he thought to himself? A young nephew would be more romantically inclined and perhaps bold enough to encourage true love. Did he not know and endorse 'Amor omnia vincit'?

He approached the King by sending a message through his bribed servant in which he asked him whom, he Sudeley should marry.

'Your Majesty' said the King's servant approaching the young Edward with some diffidence. 'I have a message here for from Lord Sudeley to which he begs an answer'. On reading the request from Sudeley Edward was not a little puzzled but put his mind to the answer. Edward (perhaps he had a sense of humour) advised that he should marry Anne of Cleves. His second choice would be the Princess Mary! Thomas laughed quietly to himself at the thought of wedding the ugly Lady Anne despite her properties which held attractions. Even if he could steel himself to approach Anne he thought she would most probably have a tart and withering answer for him. There was also the problem of her lingering body odours.

He shivered slightly at the thought of wedding the Princess Mary with her decided religious beliefs and haunted and unattractive personality. Did the King really mean to be serious? Sudeley, nothing daunted, approached the King once more through his servant and this time was more direct in his question. 'Your Majesty I much respect Queen Anne of Cleves but have it on good authority that the Queen will not taste of marriage again. I beg you to answer me in your wisdom as to the possibility of marrying the Queen Katherine, the widow of your late lamented King and father'. He also sent a supply of gold which he knew was denied to the King and the answer came back as he desired it. 'I wish you much joy of my beloved Mother Queen if she agrees in her sadness to recover her spirits by marrying you.'

Katharine by this time had effected her removal to the large house in Old Chelsea which had been built by the late King for his Queen Jane Seymour. It was a spacious and beautiful Tudor building very much in the style of Henry's other grand building, St James's Palace. Sudeley had visited his late sister's intended residence some time before and considered it a very fitting place for him to hopefully assure his abode in town. He did not doubt that the Queen Katharine would be amenable to his companionship. She needed cheering up and he was the very man to do it.

At the same time the ambitious Sudeley had his own secret plans for the marriage of the young King which he had hinted to Katharine. He turned to the Marquess of Dorset whose daughter Jane Grey was about the King's age and was named after Sudeley's own sister the Queen Jane Seymour. There was much to encourage the plan in Sudeley's book as he knew that

Jane would be glad to escape the unforgiving parenting of her mother and father. Jane would have access to the King's excellent tutors to complete her education and Sudeley would compensate himself for not being on the Council by having immediate access to the King. How sad for poor Jane Grey that this furtive plan did not see the light of day as then she would have avoided the ghastly death which lay in wait for her on the scaffold. Her father scotched the plan, feeling that Sudeley was a man of straw who had schemes above his ability to realise them. He sent him a tart message.

'To my Lord Sudeley upon his request for the hand of my daughter Jane to wed His Majesty. I do not think My Lord that as you are not a member of the Council, it would lie in your jurisdiction to order the marriage of His Majesty. My daughter Lady Jane is young and has her studies to complete. I beg in all sincerity to thank you for the suggestion which I must hereby refute.' He may be Lord High Admiral and Baron Sudeley but he could not possibly arrange the marriage of the King from the sidelines. Dorset was a man of iron will as his daughter was well aware and he turned his back on Sudeley's scheme as impractical and undesirable. Even if he had not done so it was inevitable that the Council would never have allowed a Council outsider to plan the future matrimonial course of the King. To place power and influence in the hands of such a man was not to be taken seriously. Even the undoubted attraction of having Jane's education under the auspices of the learned Queen Katharine did not convince her father.

Sudeley shrugged his shoulders and smiled to himself. There would be other fathers eager to place their daughter in the way of the King and under the tutorship of the blue stocking Katharine who would doubtless have abetted his plan willingly. Perhaps some fathers would even have greased the palms of the Council to sweeten their ambitions. Who knew? He was not finished yet.

'My dear Thomas' said Katharine. 'I am so sorry that the Marquess did not approve your plan of which you now inform me. Jane is, I believe, a strong minded young lady with a keen interest in learning. It would have completed my happiness to guide her path to womanhood and perhaps the throne. She would have been a gift to compensate me for my own sad lack of offspring.' Thomas replied calmly 'I would have thought the recommendation of the widow of the late King would have been enough to sway the Council. It seems that that counts for nothing nowadays'. Katharine was not a little upset by this terse summary of her influence and despite her age and experience the odd tear fell from her eye. Did her new lover only value her for her influence? Was she really wise to ally herself to one so lacking in feeling? Katharine turned away so as not to let Sudeley see that he had wounded her. Perhaps she would be happier on her own after all? Her own mother had lived as a widow for many years without too much grief as she supposed. Was she rash to throw away the chance of real freedom for the first time in her life? And yet Sudeley had a powerful attraction for her and life and company were more amenable with a partner or husband as support. Also she had to admit – this was certainly her last chance of love and with such a charismatic man. She swallowed her pride and turned to him with a smile on her face.

'Have no fear my dear Katharine' he said. 'He will live to regret his antipathy. Lady Jane Grey could have enjoyed a glittering future'. He put his arm round her shoulders and kissed her lightly on the cheek.

'Well Thomas my dear, I have other concerns at the moment and must leave this problem for you to solve. My goods are now all moved today and I am to sleep tonight in my new home. All that remains for me to do is to choose those personal objects of clothing that belonged to King Henry. He also left me valuable jewels which I must view another day. You can be assured that they are not resting permanently with Anne Somerset. Tonight I sleep at Chelsea, my own mistress and away from the court. I will leave you now and will retire to my residence and God be with you'. With a parting kiss she swept out of the room and Thomas turned away to ponder on his next move. He had been thwarted in the Jane Grey episode but he had other plans of a personal and more important nature for his future well being.

The week after Katharine's removal to Chelsea he visited her and was greeted warmly with a kiss which he prolonged in embracing her.

'Well my dear Katharine, how do you like being the mistress of this grand house and will you show me round the house and the gardens?' Katharine was only too pleased to walk out into the courtyard garden with Thomas and together they sat on a seat and enjoyed the first rays of spring sunshine.

'How I have missed you Katharine' he said slipping his arm around her shoulders.

'Indeed dear Thomas I am now my own mistress and can order my own life for the first time.'

'J would that that life would include me in it' said Thomas kissing her cheek.

'His late Majesty was not averse to me re-marrying' she said. 'Indeed he expected it for he left me a generous sum of money if I should take that step. I have thought about this for many a long hour and have decided that my happiness lies with you'.

This was music to Thomas's ears as it was the first he had heard of this monetary incentive to his plans.

'That wish makes me the happiest of mortal men' smiled Thomas and lifted her hand to his lips. 'However the Council would have to be told and may not approve. The Lord Protector would have to agree if the young King did, but you know his wife Anne hates me and will do all in her power to obstruct our plans. She is a bitter and unforgiving woman'

'Then we shall marry secretly here in my own home' said Katharine. 'It will be clandestine and in the early morning. I will meet the King alone tomorrow if possible and request his definite approval. He has ever been my friend and will not, I think, deny me. He knows his father foresaw an event of this sort. The Princesses may be more difficult. I know the Princess Mary is very close to your brother the Lord Protector's wife Anne who served the King's first Spanish queen. I know Anne bears me no love and will poison her husband the Protector's mind against me. It seems that Anne knows well how to hate but little of love. The Princess Elizabeth knows that I have mentioned the subject of her living with me and the Council do not disapprove of that. I will renew my proposal and ask her to decide if she will come to Old Chelsea and if she agrees the Council can hardly deny her. She is not close to the succession. First of all I must seek a private audience with the King and if he gives me his definite royal approval to our secret marriage I will beg him not to divulge our plans just yet. In respect of the death of the King his father not three months ago, I will tell him our wish to keep the celebration private and secret. All that I wish for as a wedding gift is his approval. Tomorrow I will go and then I will write to my sister and request that you may stay with her for a time as you will not be able to live here until the Council approves.' Thomas looked crestfallen but had to agree with the wisdom of Katharine's plans. Katharine turned to him with a loving smile. 'For the first time in my life I can choose my destiny. I have had three good and kind husbands chosen for me and have had more good fortune than any woman could dream of. But now I will wed you Thomas as the husband I have freely chosen and with the wisdom of years know that I choose rightly. I will write to my sister immediately that you may stay with her soon. Nay do not kiss me for walls have ears and eyes and discretion must be our motto. I shall miss you as you know but it cannot be for long and we will only write to each other every two weeks.'

'As you wish my love. Time will pass by on leaden feet.' He glanced up at Katharine and decided to take the plunge in asking her something that worried him. 'I know this is not my concern' he began 'but I heard talk that the Protector's wife Anne is planning to remove your jewels from the Tower permanently as she says she is entitled to them since her husband is the real ruler of the land until Edward's majority'.

'The King, may God bless his soul left me my jewels with his dying breath' said Katharine. 'Anne is a jealous woman but now is not the time to challenge her. We must first of all be careful to keep ourselves quiet without attracting attention. That problem we can address when we are married. Anne is mainly concerned that I have precedence over her and whilst she is married to a Duke she will never be a queen. She is a small minded woman.'

Thomas and Katharine looked over the rooms on the ground floor and Thomas liked what he saw. He could not wait to be master of this stately dwelling. He would be almost able to feel himself then, a king by proxy.

'I will hear from the Princess Elizabeth soon I hope and will keep you in touch with her definite answer.' Thomas happily nodded his approval as they parted company for some little time.

However Thomas found it too difficult to keep his distance from his distinguished love and slipped off whenever he could to visit her under the cloak of darkness. Katharine's sister was aware that he was probably leading another life and asked him about his whereabouts, when she could tactfully bring the subject up. Thomas related the least offensive of his whereabouts, including his visit to the Princess Elizabeth and the Princess Mary though he rather doubted that she believed him.

Elizabeth was happy to definitely accede to the suggestion that she set up house with Katharine and said that this was the very outcome she had planned and dreamed of. Mary, as Sudeley supposed, gave him a chilly stare and said that she would live with no-one but a fellow Catholic. However she was quite content to live at Windsor if she were so permitted and that her brother the King would have his own preferences when it came to her permanent abode. She preferred at this time to live in the country where no-one could interfere with her wish to follow her true faith as she saw it. In keeping faith with Catholicism she was also keeping faith with her mother's homeland.

Meanwhile Katherine made preparations for her marriage in Chelsea and chose a priest she could trust to perform the ceremony without announcing it to the wide world. She advised the young King of her actions and he duly recorded this in his private diary. It was still not four months since the death of King Henry and many would be shocked if they knew of her rapid change of affections. They might well condemn a wife who wept copiously for her dying husband and then almost immediately transferred her affections to another man.

She confided in Thomas 'if the Lord Protector and his wife do not like the marriage it will be of no consequence'. He in his turn took private delight in imagining the annoyance of the couple and their impotence to prevent it. This he felt was some compensation for not being on the Council. Now he would take precedence over his old adversary Duchess Anne or so he thought. She however, was not finished with him nor with Katharine and suspected her probable alliance with Sudeley.

'How shall it be if the King's widow produces a child so shortly after his death?' she demanded of her husband. He, who was of a less pernicious personality than his wife, shrugged his shoulders.

'If the Queen Katharine should produce a royal child it would be a miracle' he said. 'The King was in no fit state to lie with the Queen for some time before his sad death and with the addition of the four months since then there is no sign of Queen Katharine showing signs of being with child. Do not concern yourself, dear wife, with things that cannot be prevented and are really of no concern of ours.'

'They are certainly a concern for the morality of the court' retorted his wife but she was met with a half smile which further angered her but to which she had no valid remonstrance.

Rumours floated round about the probability of Sudeley's plans but nothing definite was known and Sudeley's prime concern was to keep the King aloof from the fallout of the conspiracy for the time being.

. He also had to contend with Katherine's brother Lord Essex who, although of a mild disposition, still thought fit to employ spies. He could be roused to anger as had been seen with the affair of his wife. That way trouble lay.

Katharine was defiant at this juncture saying 'If the Protector and his wife do not like this marriage it will be of no concern. If my brother objects it is of no consequence.'

At last the King called the Lord Protector in as Katherine intimated that the knowledge was being rumoured around.

'My lord I wish you to know something which to this day has been kept secret but of which I feel sure you will approve'.

'Tell me Your Majesty, I am eager to learn'.

'Then you must know that I agreed with the marriage of my stepmother Queen Katharine to my uncle Thomas and I wish them a long and happy life together'.

'Indeed Your Majesty I am much surprised and also would have liked to have been consulted'.

'There was no need my Lord Protector as I gave permission as King'. Edward waited for the outburst but none came.

'As Your Majesty wishes though I am always on hand to advise you'.

'Indeed Sir and I would ask your advice if I thought it necessary. As my dear Mother Queen was expected to remarry by my late father King Henry he left a large sum of money to her for this end, which I wish you to disburse to her'. The Lord Protector bowed his head to hide his expression of disapproval and backed his way out of the room. Edward drew a deep breath of satisfaction and turned back to his books. His father would have expected him to act as a king should and to make his wishes known and respected despite his tender years. He was not an athletic youngster and his frail constitution meant that he was happier in his studies than at the tilting yard. However his deep affection for Katharine made him her ally in whatever she chose in the way of contentment.

    For her part Katharine found an unexpected delight in the apparent unorthodoxy of the situation as it was a novelty for her. She felt that whatever the disapprovals she aroused, she was nevertheless an independent woman in charge of her own destiny for a change. She wrote to Sudeley 'I would not have you think that this, mine honest goodwill towards you, proceeds from any sudden motion of passion, for as truly as God is God, my mind was fully bent the other time I was at liberty to marry you before any man I know. Howbeit, God withstood my will therein most vehemently for a time and through his grace and goodness, made that seem possible which seemed to me most impossible: that made me renounce utterly my own will and follow His most willingly. It were long to write all the process of this matter. If I live I shall declare it to you myself. I can say nothing but – as my Lady of Suffolk says – God is a marvellous man. By her that is yours to serve and obey during life, Katharine the Queen. KP

Sudeley, who was still living with Katharine's sister replied to her 'For by her company in default of yours, I shall shorten the weeks in these parts, which heretofore were three days longer than they were under the planets at Chelsea.' He intended, he said, to obtain the goodwill of his brother and the Council if possible and he asked the Queen to send him a miniature of herself. He signed himself 'Him whom you have bound to honour, love and in all lawful things to obey'.

Sudeley wrote to his brother the Lord Protector requesting a meeting and determining to unburden his breast to him and hopefully win his sympathy, but the Lord Protector deferred the meeting. Sudeley was worried that there was trouble brewing and wrote to Katherine. 'As you see fit my love, do you press the Lord Protector with all speed to make known our union for I much regret my absence from your loving presence'. Katherine was also anxious to be united with her husband and saw no reason for continued secrecy. 'If the Lord Protector delays longer the news of our wedding, known to the King, it will be mooted to others also. This would bring disfavour on the Seymour family in a manner not to be an advantage to them. If your brother continues to harbour in secrecy that which we would have known it would be better to beg the King to write endorsing our marriage and giving it his hearty approval and that of members of the Privy Council. If they do so your brother and his wife will feel obliged to also approve it'. Still she cautioned him to make his next visit secretly and early and to leave by seven in the evening. He should advise her of the time of his arrival in order that she might wait to let him in by the field gate. Katharine, always nobly wed, was reduced to the adolescent schemings of a young lover and was willing to put up with it for the passion of her life. Eventually nearly five months after the death of King Henry the Lord Protector agreed to come and dine with the Queen at Chelsea. With unaccustomed nervousness Katharine rehearsed how she would break the news of her marriage to him. Having dined him well she turned to him and said 'My Lord and honoured friend, I have something to tell you that I am bold enough to think may already be known to you'.

'What is that Queen Katharine?' said he being perhaps deliberately obtuse.

 'It is perhaps no secret to you that your brother and I are in the eyes of God and by His holy ordinance man and wife'. She drew a breath and glanced up at him trying to judge his possible reaction.

'I have suspected this for some little time' said he. 'What do you think His late Majesty would have made of it? He may perhaps have expected you to wed but not in this manner or to this person and with such unseemly haste.

'I cannot think that he would have disapproved my marrying the King's own uncle. If not he, then whom?'

'The King expressly forbade him from being on the Council. Why do you think that was?'

'That I cannot say my Lord as he did not confide in me the reason for his appointments. Lord Sudeley was given diplomatic postings and was entrusted with diplomatic secrets. He was also entrusted with the overall control of the navy. Was that not a great honour?' 'No doubt it was, but the King would not trust him to govern. And do you know this My Lady, that with his dying breath the King shouted 'no, no, no' when it was suggested that he should be on the Council.' The Protector set his jaw and said no more. After a few minutes he looked coldly at Katharine and said 'The King must be told of this'. Katharine also paused before replying 'His Majesty knows and approves'.

Somrset made to rise from the table and thanked Katharine for the meal saying that he must see the King and also the Council.' He made little conversation more before taking his leave.

On the next day he visited the King in a controlled but vexatious mood. The King wrote in his diary later 'The Lord Protector was much offended'. Nor was he alone for the Council were enraged and showed their emotions in different and unseemly ways; none were well pleased. They returned to their old theme of the possible pregnancy of Katharine which if true would pose the question of whose babe it was. 'Bring in Lord Sudeley' they demanded.

When two days later Sudeley attended the Council meeting he received nothing in the way of congratulations and much by way of indignities. They fired hostile questions at him, demanding firstly if the King had approved. When he replied in the affirmative they then sought to cast doubt on the validity of the marriage but none would stick. They had to accept in their fury that the marriage was valid and could not be rescinded. They broke up still bubbling with indignation and the Lord Protector returned to his house to ride out the wrath of his wife.

Spiteful at the best of times, now she had good reason to storm.

'Have you no authority over Lord Sudeley these days?' she demanded.

'He is of age Anne and does not need my approval. He received that of the King and that is all that was needed'. He did not add that the King was very content that his dear Mother Queen had found happiness with his much loved uncle who was delightfully liberal with gold.

Not only was the King pleased he wrote to Katharine wishing her joy and a happy marriage and thanking her for all her letters. He also thanked her for 'the great love' she had shown to his late father and her kindness at all times to himself. He admired her he said for her 'godliness and knowledge in learning and the scriptures'. His closing testimonial to her was to promise that if there was anything 'wherein I may do you a kindness, either in word or deed I will do it'. What more could Katharine have wished than to have such words from her beloved King? Edward showed that he was very much his father's son and could stand up for himself in true Tudor fashion.

In response to Katharine's pleading he told the Council that he had known and approved Katharine's wedding plans for some time and that he thoroughly approved of her action. Not only that but he had requested that Katherine should so marry leaving them to grumble impotently about the young King's attitude. What he did not divulge was that Sudeley had passed over to him considerable amounts of gold to reinforce his wishes and relieve Edward's shortage of means.

The Council bubbled with indignation, some questioning whether a minor could be trusted to act sensibly.

'The young King is headstrong' said one.

'But he knows his mind in all things' said another. 'Think how he has insisted on Protestant services in the churches and has forbidden imagery and religious icons!'

'He is as determined as his father the late King was' said another shaking his head.

Somerset addressed the Council who looked distinctly displeased with the turn of events. 'My fellow Councillors we were entrusted by the late King to manage affairs of state until King Edward reached years of discretion. However he did not ask us to rule against the King's wishes and indeed we would none of us presume to do so.' He looked around the table at the glum faces and searched in vain for one face which showed happy acquiescence.

'The King has made his wishes known and it is not for us to contravene them. Indeed would we really wish to? What would we have thought if Her Majesty had decided to wed some foreign power who might be a force of contention to us in ways unknown? Let us forget our previous wishes and accept what has occurred with good grace'. There was a subdued muttering of agreement and Somerset thankfully turned to other matters.

Not everyone, however, was so compliant. Sudeley had written to Princess Mary asking her to use her influence with the Council to accept the marriage amicably and to persuade the Queen to have a public proclamation made. Princess Mary was far from pleased and replied to that effect.

'It stands least with my poor honour to be a meddler in this matter, considering whose wife her Grace was of late. If the remembrance of the King's Majesty will not suffer her to grant your suit, I am nothing able to persuade her to forget the loss of him who is very ripe in my own remembrance.' She added tartly 'being a maid I am nothing cunning'.

It was fortunate for Sudeley that he no longer needed Mary's help and could afford to ignore her rebuke. Nor could he any longer harbour thoughts of matrimony with her. Katherine had agreed that their marriage should be made known although she was sad that in doing so she probably had lost the affection of Mary for all time. Mary, feeling increasingly beleaguered in her religious beliefs, was developing that carapace of intolerance towards others which was to be the hallmark of her future reign.

Mary then turned her guns on her stepsister writing to her that she should hold herself aloof from her father's widow in order not to sully her reputation. Elizabeth was not to be hustled and was very fond of Katharine and also secretly of her new husband. Although she was by no means naive she knew an attractive man when she saw one and was not averse to her mother's choice. She replied tactfully that when she first heard of the marriage she felt 'grief' and 'affliction' at the affair. But she continued that neither of them were able 'to offer any obstacle thereto' and that the Seymours 'having got all the authority into their hands' were not to be gainsaid. She advised Mary 'to make the best of what we cannot remedy'. She owed much to Katharine and told Mary that she would 'use much tact in manoeuvring with her, for fear of appearing ungrateful for her benefits'. She added 'I shall not however, be in any hurry to visit her lest I should be charged with approving what I ought to censure'. She however, did not intend to make an enemy of Katharine and would not adopt Mary's entrenched position. She added that the Seymours were omnipotent 'having got all authority into their hands.'

Katharine now felt relief that the worst was over and she should not hide herself away as if in shame. She therefore decided with Sudeley that they should appear at court whenever their presence might be welcome. The first time she did it she looked for Dutch courage to carry her visit through. 'My dear Thomas this day is going to be a trial for me as I fear I may be snubbed'.

'Nonsense Katharine, you are still a Queen and owed the deference due to your station. Although we may not rule, our marriage is legitimate and probably anticipated by his late Majesty. It is certainly condoned by his present Majesty. Let us hold our heads high and put our trust in God'.

Katharine drew comfort from his confidence. 'I feel that now is the time to reclaim the royal jewels which are in safe keeping at the Tower. Will you please request your brother to have them brought to me now? I shall wear some this evening and feel rightfully queenly'.

However Duchess Anne had forestalled her and had the jewels removed from safe keeping and delivered for herself to wear.

'After all we are the leaders of the Council and the highest in authority below the King' she claimed. Her husband was not so sanguine but being a peaceful man on the whole he was not one to seek battle with the termagent Anne. However battle it was until the jewels were delivered to his wife and the delay caused Seymour to openly accuse Anne of lèse-majesté. Herein the battle lines were drawn and Anne was nothing loathe to fight at every turn. When Katharine next came to court to her consternation she encountered Anne wearing what she considered were her own jewels until Edward took a wife. Anne determined to put the upstart in her place. She talked of how the King 'had married Katharine in his doting days when he had brought himself so low by his lust and cruelty that no lady who stood on her honour would venture on him'. She wrote that she would not give place to 'her who in her former estate was but Latimer's widow and is now fain to cast herself for support upon anyone who would view her with favour. 'If the Lord Protector my husband teach him no better manners I am she that will'.

Anne made her husband's life a misery until in despair he wrote to Katharine telling her that she was not able to have the jewels and that his wife took precedence. Katharine now showed she was made of sterner stuff at least with her husband who preached docility and wrote to him 'My lord you have this afternoon made me a little warm. It was fortunate we were so far distant for I suppose else I should have bitten someone. What cause have they to fear me? It is requisite for them to pray continually for a short despatch of that hell! Tomorrow or else upon Saturday I will see the King. I intend to utter all my choler to my lord and ruler'.

It would appear that Sudeley's advice was contrary and Katharine backed off from an embarrassing stand-off with the Duchess. She had to acknowledge to herself that her glory days were over and that she would have no pleasure in attending court where she would be again snubbed by Anne. She did not attend the court again and left the field clear for Anne to find another victim of her spleen.

The Sudeleys took up their residence at Chelsea whilst arranging for Sudeley Castle to be prepared for occupation in their absence. Katharine wrote to the Princess Elizabeth about her country home.

'It will give us both the greatest pleasure if your Royal Highness will do us the honour of coming to Sudeley Castle for a prolonged visit in the summer. It is a charming place and far removed from the slings and arrows of the court. If your Royal Highness should find the castle as congenial as Lord Sudeley and I do, you may consider it as you home for as long as it shall please you. A more delightful setting it is hard to imagine and the views are gentle and bewitching. There you may ride as you wish and feel the enchantment of the place where your beloved late father the King, was pleased to stay. I think the Princess Mary may perhaps visit us one day although I can only wish if her mind were so moved in that direction. If the King saw fit to visit us there our happiness would be complete, but I am not so sanguine as to that honour would be granted to him or allowed to us'.

Meanwhile at Chelsea the happy couple enjoyed their time together and Katherine invited the Princess Elizabeth to join them there. She had also suffered from the overbearing grandeur of the Lord Protector and his envious wife and she was happy enough to escape from the court.

'If you would do us the honour of residing in Chelsea I would do my utmost to further your education and to bring good tutors to your side as well as giving you of my own humble help'.

Elizabeth was quick to agree and found not only Katharine's company but also that of her new husband much to her taste.

Sudeley for his part was always ready to strengthen bonds with possible future rulers however remote that scenario may be. He also found the young Elizabeth beautiful and quick witted and ready to share his company and compliments. At a time in life when she was growing into a woman she was open to male flattery and charm as any young girl would be.

Chapter 14 The Queen in Print

He also renewed his correspondence with Lord Dorset and enquired whether Jane Grey would like to join the Princess Elizabeth in the Chelsea classroom. He still harboured the ambition of marrying the King with Lady Jane when he would then assume the chief power in the land and happily displace his brother and his ungracious wife.

'You may be assured my Lord that the opportunity for Lady Jane would be of the finest available and that the best tutors would be employed for the Princess Elizabeth as may be found and such as would not demean your daughter who is already known to be of a talented and gracious disposition.' His offer was enticing and now drew a favourable response. Sudeley then wrote that 'your daughter would have the companionship of the esteemed Princess Elizabeth in the classroom with the best tutors as promised. In addition his wife Katharine would supervise their studies being a learned lady and a published authoress.' They would both be enabled to study the scriptures and follow the Protestant religion with Katharine.

Although Sudeley was called Elizabeth's 'step-father' he could not resist flirtations which had an element of danger about them. Both step-daughter and wife found him irresistible. The sexual tension between the adolescent girl and her handsome stepfather simmered away with Katherine happily unaware of the possible dangers or repercussions. No doubt Sudeley, who was ever on 'the make' although fond of his new wife, was also increasingly drawn to her step-daughter, who was a good deal younger and in the bloom of youth. It is extraordinary that he could contemplate under the same roof physical relationships with both of them in which he might indulge with impunity. But that he attempted to do.

During her stay at Chelsea Katharine finished writing a book called 'The Lamentations of a Sinner' and no less a person than William Cecil, later to be Queen Elizabeth's chief minister, wrote the foreword in which he lauded Katharine as being 'our Queen in virtue as well as in honour'. This, Katharine's second book, was a great success and added further laurels to her reputation of which Lord Dorset was cognisant.

Not only was Katharine an acclaimed religious authoress but she found at that time the dream of her married life was about to come true as she was found to be pregnant. Fortunately it would definitely not be the child of the late King as had been much feared and discussed earlier in the Council. Katharine was at this stage past the normal time of childbearing, being into her forties. She was thrilled needless to say and began preparations for the nursery with her lady in waiting. She was so taken up with thoughts of motherhood that she failed to notice the interest her husband was taking in the young and vibrant Princess Elizabeth.

He began visiting Elizabeth in her bedroom in the morning before she had got dressed. If she were dressed he would say a few words to her and then drift off. If she were still in bed he would sit on the side of the bed in his nightshirt and lean over and kiss her and tickle her. This morning incursion took place whilst Katharine was at her prayers and also whilst her lady Mrs Ashley was still in Elizabeth's bedchamber.

'My lord I beg you not to do that' cried the young Elizabeth whilst holding her breath when he reached under the bedclothes and ran his hands over her lithe young body ending with a tickle. Elizabeth was, not for nothing, the child of the sexually voracious Henry V111 and Anne Boleyn and she was at an age when to be visited by a handsome older man in bed was both terrifying and delicious. In later life she was always attracted by handsome and dashing men such as Dudley and Essex and in younger life it was no different.

Mrs Ashley was shocked and offended and yet subject to his authority. She wrote that 'it was unseemly to see a man so little dressed in a maid's chamber'. To Elizabeth she was more direct. 'Your Royal Highness I cannot restrain myself from saying that the Admiral should consider how he offends and draw a line under such provocative and unseemly behaviour. All the time his devoted wife is at her prayers and I am fain to tell her of my fears'.

Elizabeth was enjoying hitherto forbidden fruit and did not resist when Sudeley tried to kiss her, but Mrs Ashley drove him out of the room crying 'for shame on your behaviour'. Sudeley would then make his way to the maids' bedrooms where easier pickings were available. He apparently told Katharine a part of what he was doing in order to forestall Mrs Ashley's complaints. Surprisingly Katharine did not react adversely though she must surely have had inner reservations.

An extraordinary event took place about this time which involved Katharine too. The three of them were in the garden when Sudeley came across a pair of shears which had been carelessly left behind by the gardeners. He picked them up and then made a playful gesture at Elizabeth with them, pretending to cut at her dress. Elizabeth jumped back with a shriek and ran to the distant hedge. Sudeley followed by Katharine ran after her and when Elizabeth peeped out with a squeal Sudeley caught hold of her. 'Do you my wife, cut this naughty girl's dress to teach her good manners.' Katharine playfully took a snip at the hem of the dress to Elizabeth's cries and then Sudeley grabbed the shears whilst Katharine held Elizabeth's arm and he cut several large gashes in the skirt. To the general merriment they continued to snip away at the dress until it was totally ruined. Elizabeth was by then helpless with laughter and made a dash for the house to change her garments.

Needless to say Mrs Ashley had several sharp remarks to make to Elizabeth about her behaviour with her step-father but more than that she could not say, not having witnessed the episode personally. One of the maids having heard the rumpus, observed the incident and needless to say the episode was repeated and perhaps grew in the telling.

Sudeley's morning visits continued to Mrs Ashley's disapproval and she complained again to Sudeley saying 'that my lady was evil spoken of' but the retort from Sudeley was that he would divulge how he was slandered to his brother, the Lord Protector. Mrs Ashley was not to know that Sudeley's brother would probably treat Sudeley's complaint with the contempt it deserved.

He realised he was on dangerous ground if Mrs Ashley spoke of her other fears to Katharine and he concocted a story for Katharine which was possibly fanciful. He said that he had seen Elizabeth through a window with her arms around the neck of a courtier. Katherine spoke to Mrs Ashley about this story though she knew nothing of this accusation but suggested she spoke to

Elizabeth about it. Elizabeth denied it hotly and burst into floods of tears and Katharine realised that one of the two was lying.

Katharine again sent for Mrs Ashley and confided her fears to her and asked her if she could confirm them.

'I could not say My Lady, though I feel that the Princess and the Admiral your husband are sometimes rather too familiar the one with the other. The Princess is only young and perhaps does not realise what is fitting for a young lady. As for the other accusation I know nothing about it at all.' Katharine appreciated Mrs Ashley's reluctance to cast doubt on her beloved husband and precious guest. However she asked Mrs Ashley 'to take more heed and watch betwixt the Lady Elizabeth and the Admiral'. Katharine was deeply wounded by the facts as she saw them and decided most reluctantly that she must take immediate action. She realised that an older, attractive man would be flattering to a young girl and that Elizabeth must be protected from herself.

She also turned for help to Elizabeth's financial adviser Sir Thomas Parry and discussed the matter with him. She said that 'the Admiral had loved Elizabeth too well and had done so a long while'. It cost Katharine dear to have to make this admission to a retainer and she was deeply upset. He undertook to keep his eyes open.

It was, however, Katharine herself who found out the depth of her husband's deceit. One day in summer she looked for him in vain and realised that Elizabeth too was missing. She set about searching the large house room by room from the ground floor upwards until she eventually caught them red handed embracing in the attic. Elizabeth cried out in consternation and Sudeley began to make his explanations which Katherine did not stay to hear.

She called Mrs Ashley in and maintaining her dignity despite the shock, spoke calmly to her. 'Mrs Ashley I have come across something which I am loathe to describe and all I can say is that I am deeply disappointed in the conduct of the Lady Elizabeth. She has acted disgracefully and she can no longer stay under my roof.' She forbore to accuse her husband but no doubt Mrs Ashley would draw her own conclusions from what she had seen hitherto. Mrs Ashley asked no questions but could imagine something of the situation. Katharine for her part, remained dignified and outwardly calm and bore her pain with resignation. She did not berate her husband, neither did she speak to him but he got wind of the approaching and probable scandal and when he tried to offer some sort of excuse she swept out of the room silently.

It was Mrs Ashley, not Katharine, who told the Princess that they were asked to leave Chelsea. She did not state the reason but Elizabeth, in tears, said that 'she had loved the Admiral too well.' Mrs Ashley took her in her arms and held her close but said nothing. She sympathised with the frailty of a young adolescent and privately condemned the irresponsible and deceitful behaviour of the Admiral.

Katharine called Elizabeth to her before she left for her own house in Cheston. She did not mention the affair but gave Elizabeth some parting words of advice.

'God has given you great qualities. Cultivate them always and labour to improve them, for I believe you are destined by Heaven to be Queen of England.' Elizabeth kissed her; unable to speak in the face of Katharine's stony expression and she took her leave. The incident affected Katherine deeply as she had loved Elizabeth as a daughter but inwardly she blamed her husband who was old enough to know better.

Katherine was now left to share her house and her life with a proven philanderer as a husband and the atmosphere was decidedly chilly. When she spoke to Sudeley he tried to revarnish his reputation by saying that he was very sorry for what had happened but that Elizabeth had led him on and encouraged him. He was never loathe to lay the blame elsewhere and to tarnish a young girl's reputation which did not enhance him in his wife's estimation. Katherine knew this to be untrue and was now facing life with a liar as well as a molester. With great dignity she forbore to enter into arguments and rancorous scenes which would lead nowhere. When she was left alone with her own thoughts she looked back on her earlier marriages and certainly the first two, as being a good deal easier and pleasanter. However the thought of divorce was one which appalled her and she bravely faced the future with what was left of their relationship.

When Elizabeth reached Cheston Mrs Ashley made an extraordinary confession to her. 'My lady I am led to believe that the Admiral would have married you if he had been allowed to rather than taking the step he did.' Elizabeth stared at her in disbelief. 'How can you possibly know that Mrs Ashley?'

'I know it well from what others have said and from my own realisation.' In fact although Sudeley may have so wished, there is no way that the Council would have endorsed his plan and the two would have been parted. Elizabeth sat down suddenly in shock. Worse was to come for walls have ears and one of the servants overheard this exchange and dashed off to the servants' quarters to gabble out the news. Word spread and soon it was common knowledge much to Katharine's grief. As is usual gossip acquired its own plethora of additions and there was public chatter about the doings of the Princess and the Admiral, some even saying that a child had been secretly born and smuggled away. When she did indeed become sick and took to her bed the rumours grew even stronger but they proved baseless and Elizabeth behaved with dignity, neither speaking of the rumours nor denying them. The end of the affair came with a letter from the Admiral who absolved Elizabeth from any blame and promised to testify to her innocence if need be. It was a cold document and he received an equally detached letter in reply from Elizabeth.

'You need not send an excuse to me' she wrote, ending 'I pray you give my commendations to the Queen's Highness'. She added 'I commit you and your affairs into God's hand'.

She was deeply mortified that she had caused Katherine such lasting hurt and she was to bear the scars for the remainder of her life, conducting herself in the days to come so as to be above recriminations. Her reputation was henceforth to be her guiding light and she was fortunate that her succession to the throne was not called in doubt.

Chapter 15   The Final Betrayal

When she did accede to the throne and was lionised by handsome and dashing men such as Dudley and Essex, she took the utmost care that her conduct though teasing and flirtatious at times, never crossed the barrier of scandal or immorality. Her father's example had fortified her against marriage and Sudeley's had prevented her from going beyond flirtation. She was condemned by her own perspicacity from being other than the Virgin Queen.

By this time it was perhaps as well that Sudeley Castle was ready for occupation and Katharine hoped that the move would restrict her husband's activities with regard to philanderings which involved the court and its denizens. Perhaps the running of the castle and country activities would be enough to occupy him constructively.

Before their decision to move the King has written to Katharine telling her not to fear a backlash from anyone regarding her marriage. He promised her that 'I will so provide for you both that if hereafter any grief befall, I shall be a sufficient succour in your godly and praisable enterprises'. They must have both found this kindly and reassuring but In effect he was kept under close scrutiny and had been unable to help his stepmother recover her jewels. His kindness to Katharine was a great source of comfort to her however, when she was feeling saddened and beleaguered and she knew he wished her well. It was not his last letter to her though as he said he rarely 'had half an hour alone'. Sudeley continued to ensure that he had sufficient pocket money and that he still figured in the King's mind. Perhaps he still nursed a hope that he would in time marry Jane Grey and that then he would be a power in the land as his brother was now.

The Lord Protector was relieved that the couple were away from the court and did not provide further fuel for his wife's contentious flames. In gratitude he made Sudeley Captain General and Protector's Lieutenant in the south of England. Although these were but honorary appointments they signalled his affection for the couple and perhaps his relief that they were moving to Gloucestershire.

It was to Katharine's great joy that she found that she was pregnant and the event that she had longed for during three previous marriages looked likely to occur. It came at a good time when she and Sudeley were striving to put their marriage on a firm and hopefully happy footing.

Whilst he was back at court temporarily fulfilling duties connected with his appointments Katharine felt the child moving and with delight wrote to her husband. "Sweetheart and loving husband,

I gave your little knave your blessing, who like an honest man stirred apace after and before; for Mary Odell my midwife, being abed with me, laid her hand on my belly to feel it stir. It has stirred these here days every morning and evening, so that I trust when you come it will make you some pastime. And thus I end, bidding my sweetheart and loving husband better to fare than myself'.

Sudeley replied that it 'had revived' his spirits.' He was still badgering his brother for the return of Katharine's jewels. He was trying his best to reinstate himself in Katharine's good opinion by regaining the treasures and said; as regards the baby 'If God should give him a life as long as his father's he will revenge such wrongs as neither you nor I can at present.' He said that he had spoken so forcefully to his brother that he had said 'you shall either have your own again or else some recompense as you shall be content withal'.

Thomas gave his wife some sound advice 'to keep the little knave so lean and gaunt with your good diet and walking that he may be so small that he may creep out of a mouse hole. And I bid my most dear and well beloved wife most heartily to fare. Your Highness most faithful loving husband   Thomas Seymour.'

When back in Gloucestershire they had news from the King that the Duchess of Somerset had been delivered of a son to be named after her husband which gave Katherine comfortable hopes of her own confinement.

She also received a letter from Elizabeth which was a thinly veiled bid for forgiveness. She said she thanked her 'for the manifold kindnesses at your Highness' hand at my departure' reiterating that 'truly I was replete with sorrow to depart from Your Highness. I weighed it deeply when you said that you should warn me of all evilness that you should hear of me; for if your Grace had not a good opinion of me, you would not have offered friendship to me that way at all.
Your Highness's humble daughter, Elizabeth'.

Katharine was not one to bear grudges especially against a young girl and wrote back a warm letter protesting her support and amity.

Elizabeth was much relieved to be forgiven and wrote that her reply was 'most joyful to me'. She added that she was glad that

Katharine was so enjoying Sudeley Castle and she rejoiced to hear 'how the busy child doth; if I were at his birth, no doubt I would see him beaten for the trouble he hath put you to'. She ended 'giving Your Highness most humble thanks for your commendations'.

Never again could Elizabeth be trusted to share a house with Katharine but another interesting and in time tragic person did come to stay with her. Jane Grey's family had been somewhat besieged by Sudeley's requests for Jane to join them although there was no longer the attraction of lessons to be had with Elizabeth. It was perhaps fortunate that they did not know the affair of Elizabeth or his infatuation with pubescent daughters.

When Jane rode into the drive at Sudeley Castle it was a beautiful sunny day and she was enchanted with the surroundings. She was a serious young lady much on her dignity and not one Sudeley would have contemplated romping with.

'Your Highness I am so honoured to visit you' she said curtseying to Katharine and kissing her hand. Katherine embraced her warmly and was delighted to have a young companion to replace Elizabeth.

'We shall have some delightful explorations round the grounds Jane and you can help me to plan the garden and name your favourite flowers. You may like to climb the tower sometime from where you will have a superb view though I shall not ascend all those steps this time.' Jane was shown her chamber with its delightful view and Katharine took her to the little room which she had arranged for the new baby's nursery. During her stay the two ladies became firm friends and Jane was to Katharine the daughter she never had. Together they read the

Bible and studied ancient history and literature. For Katharine, Jane, the serious blue stocking was the ideal young companion.

It may have been as well that Katharine did not live to see the tragic end to Jane's short life when she was executed for something of which she was entirely guiltless.

Katharine with Jane beside her was happy to welcome the many friends who arrived from London to visit the Sudeley's country estate though the Duke and Duchess of Somerset were notable absentees. The welcome to their visitors was almost on a royal scale as they were not short of money to fund their lavish lifestyle. Among Katharine's visitors she was particularly delighted to welcome old friends from former days who knew so well Katharine's former queenly days of yore at court.

A further joy in Katharine's life was to receive a friendly letter from the Princess Mary brought by Katharine's brother William. Mary had disapproved of Katharine's remarriage at first but at last the ice had thawed and she wrote that 'I hope to hear good news of Your Grace's great belly and in the meantime shall desire much to hear of your good health.' She signed herself 'Your Grace's humble and assured loving daughter'. It seemed that all was well with Katharine's new world at last. The kind letter of Mary belies her icy character and gave Katherine great joy.

Katharine's daughter was born on August 30 1548 and was christened 'Mary' after the Princess Mary. Elizabeth may have had a pang of guilt when she heard of the choice of name.

Sudeley would have preferred a son but was nevertheless delighted that a baby girl had arrived and notified his brother Somerset forthwith.

He received a friendly letter back though with no felicitations included from the intractable Anne. He wrote 'I am right glad to understand from your letters that the Queen, your bedfellow, hath a happy hour, and, escaping all danger, hath made you the father of so pretty a daughter; and although (if it had pleased God) it would have been both to us and (we suppose) also to you more joy and comfort if it had, this first-born, been a son, yet the escape of the danger, and the prophecy of this to a great sort of happy sons is no small joy and comfort to us, as we are sure it is to you and her Grace also, to whom you shall make again our hearty commendations, with no less congratulation of such good success, from your loving brother, E Somerset.'

Apparently Somerset's wife had failed to add her congratulations because she, Katharine had only had a daughter whereas she had recently produced a son.

Sadly Katharine's joy was not to last as she developed puerperal fever and was not in her right mind for the week following the birth. When Thomas sat by her bedside he was alarmed to hear Katharine say 'and where is my husband Lord Sudeley and where is the Princess Elizabeth, tell me that if you will. They are together making light of their vows in a room where they thought not to be found.'

Thomas dismissed the nurses from the room as Katharine raved in her fever and allowed them back when she had fallen asleep. Yet still Katharine kept tossing and turning and calling out such things as 'Elizabeth be off with you and do not trouble my husband any more'. It was not surprising that despite their mutual protestations of friendship, Elizabeth and Katharine never met at Sudeley Castle.

One day when Lady Tyrwhitt entered Katharine's room she was met with the enquiry as to where she had been for such a long time. She added that 'she did fear such things in herself that she was sure she could not live.' Lady Tyrwhitt tried to comfort her but Katharine rambled on

'There they are in each other's arms as I found them. Did you ever know a wife so callously treated by her loving husband? I see my Lord Latimer trying to speak to me. I have been shamelessly treated by her and my husband.'

As Sudeley sat by her bedside she held his hand saying 'Lady Tyrwhitt I am not well handled, for those that are about me care not for me, but stand laughing at my grief, and the more good I will to them, the less good they will to me'.

Lady Tyrwhitt was of course shocked to hear this which was news to her. Sudeley hastily tried to stop her speaking saying 'Why sweetheart, I would do you no hurt'.

Katharine replied in agony, 'No my lord, I think so'. He leant closer to her to hear her whispered words 'But my lord, you have given me many shred taunts'. The Admiral pretended not to hear her saying 'she is indeed raving' but Lady Tyrwhitt remembered afterwards that Katharine spoke 'with good memory and very sharply and earnestly for her mind was sore disquieted.'

To soothe her Thomas lay on the bed beside her and put his arms around her trying to calm her and if possible divert her agonised thoughts. But Katharine was not to be quieted and said 'My lord I would have given a thousand marks to have had my full talk with the doctor the first day I was delivered, but I durst not for fear of displeasing you'. Lady Tyrwitt tactfully withdrew out of earshot but she recalled afterwards that Katharine wildly berated her husband for an hour or more. Eventually the fever abated and Katharine realising that she was dying dictated her will.

'I Katharine Parr, lying on my death-bed, sick of body but of good mind and perfect memory and discretion, being persuaded and perceiving the extremity of death to approach me, give all to my married spouse and husband, wishing them to be a thousand times more in value than they are or have been'.

The will was signed by her doctor and steward and Katharine died the following morning before dawn. Lady Jane Grey came to see her as she lay dying but Katharine did not recognise her. Lady Jane sat weeping by the bedside of her friend and mentor who had been so good and kind to her. She had loved Katharine more than her own termagent mother to whom she would have to return before too long.

Katharine was embalmed and dressed in rich clothes before being placed in a lead coffin. Her husband, racked with guilt, tried to ensure that her burial would be given all dignities. She was given a funeral with all pomp and reverence with Jane Grey being the chief mourner. Sudeley did not attend the service as was the custom. Katherine was laid beneath the stones before the altar; the guests took their leave and Sudeley was left alone in a bleak and unforgiving castle with his regrets and memories.

The actors also in this drama played out the rest of their lives largely in tragedy. Jane Grey went to the scaffold being the innocent pawn in Protestant hands trying to place her on the throne instead of Mary.

Seymour was himself executed for being found near the King's bedroom at night though his motives were not divulged.

Katharine's burial chamber was neglected and workmen found her rotting coffin during restoration of the chapel many years later. Her skin was intact but crumbled on contact with the air. Sudeley Castle to this day is imbued with the memory of this Queen whose life was often happy but largely sad. It is as well that Katherine did not witness her husband's demise nor that of her devoted and deeply religious Jane Grey.

King Edward died young but ensured England's religion as being largely Protestant and only Elizabeth's life ended in triumph as Gloriana, the epitome of royal splendour. The hard lessons she had learnt in her formative years stood Elizabeth in good stead as perhaps the most revered ruler in England's long and chequered history.

Sudeley Castle endures still in its glorious setting but owing to the work of Cromwell's Puritan army suffered devastation to its Tudor splendour; but there are intact corners of Katherine's rooms where her spirit may linger in perpetuity mourning her deceased infant.

Printed in Great Britain
by Amazon